Praise for C

"Mr. O'Kelly hoped that by ....   leave behind a lesson on how to die. He did that, yes, but he also left a lesson on how to live."

—Lisa Belkin, *New York Times*

"Voicing universal truths . . . shared . . . simply and clearly."

—Janet Maslin, *New York Times*

"The meditations on turning ordinary experiences into 'perfect moments' is perhaps the most useful guidance he offers those not yet facing the timetable he confronted. Finding perfection in the mundane is a skill too many leave undeveloped, and undervalued."

—Celia Dean, *New York Times*

"Eugene O'Kelly made a generous gift of this book. He left behind something wise and insightful; it's something we all can use."

—Paul Newman

"Poignant memoir . . . gives readers words to live by."

—*USA Today*

"[A] well-written and moving book."

—The Economist.com

"An honest, thought-provoking memoir. . . . O'Kelly has many lessons to teach us on how to live."

—Steve Powers, *Houston Chronicle*

"Provides a surprising lesson in the art of living."

—Richard Pachter, *Miami Herald*

"This book is his gift to us."
—*Toronto Globe & Mail*

"One of the most unexpected and touching books
you're likely to read this year."
—Edward Nawotka, *Bloomberg News*

"Inspirational"
—*Newsday*

"This is a book that needs to be read by all of us
who think that we have a chance to slow down later.
I can't remember being moved by a book like I am
being moved by this book."
—Jack Covert, CEO Read Blog

"A few weeks ago, a book was published that has
as much power to change people's lives . . .
as does any tale of addiction/recovery. . . .
Chasing Daylight is a remarkable book."
—Bethanne Patrick, AOL's Book Maven

"Three months before he died, Eugene O'Kelly
was one of the most powerful businessmen in America.
Then he was told he had brain cancer.
In a moving memoir he describes what his preparations
for death taught him about life."
—*The Times of London*

"A calm, moving account of one person's preparations
for death. . . . This little book makes an enormous—
and enormously positive—impact."
—*Accounting and Business*, Stefan Stern

CHASING DAYLIGHT

CHASING DAYLIGHT

How My Forthcoming Death Transformed My Life

A final account

Eugene O'Kelly

with Andrew Postman

New York   Chicago   San Francisco   Lisbon
London   Madrid   Mexico City   Milan   New Delhi
San Juan   Seoul   Singapore   Sydney   Toronto

17   LCR   21

ISBN-13: 978-0071499934
ISBN-10: 0071499938

Printed and bound by Lakeside Book Company.

A portion of this book's sales will go to The Eugene O'Kelly Cancer Survivors' Fund in order to provide financial assistance to less fortunate cancer patients and their families.

Eugene O'Kelly Cancer Survivors' Fund
Schwab Fund for Charitable Giving
101 Montgomery Street
San Francisco, CA 94104
Account #: 8137-1261

For Marianne and Gina,
my greatest gifts

For Corinne,
my companion in this life,
my guide in approaching the next

Through our living room window we watched the fireworks launching from the Macy's barge on the East River. Exactly one year before, I'd seen them from the river itself, experiencing the fireworks of 2004 up close as a guest on *The Highlander*, the Forbes family yacht. At that time, I had no idea what the next year would bring, as if we ever do.

It's misleading to say I "watched" the fireworks. On this night, July 4, 2005, the real highlight—at least for me—was not visual. True, I had developed vision problems, including blurriness and blind spots, which naturally diminished the glory of the spectacle, the arc and splash of the fireworks showering the sky outside our apartment window. But even had I been able to see more clearly, the real thrill was the sound. Explosions booming off the surrounding skyscrapers, noise rumbling in the canyons of Manhattan's avenues, deep drumming like thunder reverberating throughout my body and my city. The sound was beautiful; it was eye-opening. I would never have guessed the best part of fireworks could be something besides light and color.

You never know how you'll be surprised.

Contents

FOR ANYTHING THAT MEN CAN TELL, DEATH MAY BE
THE GREATEST GOOD THAT CAN HAPPEN TO THEM:
BUT THEY FEAR IT AS IF THEY KNOW QUITE WELL
THAT IT WAS THE GREATEST OF EVILS. AND WHAT IS
THIS BUT THAT SHAMEFUL IGNORANCE OF THINKING
THAT WE KNOW WHAT WE DO NOT KNOW?

—Socrates

CHASING DAYLIGHT

A GIFT

I was blessed. I was told I had three months to live.
You think that to put those two sentences back to back,
I must be joking. Or crazy. Perhaps that I lived a miserable,
unfulfilled life, and the sooner it was done, the better.

Hardly. I loved my life. Adored my family. Enjoyed my
friends, the career I had, the big-hearted organizations I
was part of, the golf I played. And I'm quite sane. And also
quite serious: The verdict I received the last week of May
2005—that it was unlikely I'd make it to my daughter
Gina's first day of eighth grade, the opening week of
September—turned out to be a gift. Honestly.

Because I was forced to think seriously about my own
death. Which meant I was forced to think more deeply

about my life than I'd ever done. Unpleasant as it was, I forced myself to acknowledge that I was in the final stage of life, forced myself to decide how to spend my last 100 days (give or take a few weeks), forced myself to act on those decisions.

In short, I asked myself to answer two questions: *Must the end of life be the worst part?* And, *Can it be made a constructive experience—even the best part of life?*

No. Yes. That's how I would answer those questions, respectively. I was able to approach the end while still mentally lucid (usually) and physically fit (sort of), with my loved ones near.

As I said: a blessing.

Of course, almost no one thinks in detail about one's actual death. Until I had to I didn't—not really. We feel general and profound anxiety about it, but figuring out the nuts and bolts of how to make the best of one's last days, and then how to ensure that one follows the planned course of action for the benefit of oneself and one's loved ones, are not typical habits of the dying, and most certainly not of the healthy and hearty. Some people don't think about death because it comes suddenly and prematurely. Quite a few who die this way—in a car accident, say—had not yet even begun to think of themselves as mortal. My death, on the other hand, while somewhat premature (I was 53 at the time of the verdict) could not be called sudden (anyway, you couldn't call it that two weeks after the death sentence had sunk in), since I was informed quite explicitly that my final day on this Earth would happen during the 2005 calendar year.

Some people don't think about how to make the most of their last stage because, by the time their end has clearly come upon them, they are no longer in a position, mental or physical, to make of their final days what they might have. Relief of pain is their primary concern.

Not me. I would not suffer like that. Starting weeks before the diagnosis, when atypical (if largely unnoticed) things began happening to me, I had no pain, not an ounce. Later, I was told that the very end would be similarly free of pain. The shadows that had begun very slowly to darken my mind would lengthen, just as they do on the golf course in late afternoon, that magical time, my favorite time to be out there. The light would flatten. The hole—the object of my focus—would become gradually harder and harder to pick out. Eventually it would be difficult even to name. Brightness would fade. I would lapse into a coma. Night would fall. I would die.

Because of the factors surrounding my dying—my relative youth, my continued possession of mental facility and otherwise good physical health, my freedom from daily pain, and the proximity of loved ones, most of whom were themselves still in their prime—I took a different approach to my last 100 days, one that required that I keep my eyes as wide open as possible. Even with blurry vision.

Oh, yes . . . there was one more factor, probably the primary one, that influenced the way I approached my demise: my brain. The way I thought. First as an accountant, then as an ambitious businessman, and finally as the CEO of a major American firm. My sensibilities about work and accomplishment, about consistency and continuity and commitment, were so ingrained in me from my professional life, and had served me so well in that life, that I couldn't imagine *not* applying them to my final task. Just as a successful executive is driven to be as strategic and prepared as possible to "win" at everything, so I was now driven to be as methodical as possible during my last hundred days. The skill set of a CEO (ability to see the big picture, to deal with a wide range of problems, to plan for contingencies, etc.) aided me in preparing for my death. (And—not to be overlooked—my final experience taught me some things that, had I known them earlier, would have made me a better CEO and person.) In approaching my last project so systematically, I hoped to make it a positive experience for those around me, as well as the best three months of my life.

I was a lucky guy.

———— ✦ ————

Suppose I hadn't been given just 100 days. What might I have been doing?

Thinking about my next business trip, probably to Asia. Planning how to attract new business while managing the accounts we already had. Formulating initiatives for six months down the road, a year, five years. My executive calendar was always plotted out 12 to 18 months hence; it came with the job. My position demanded that I think constantly about the future. How to build on the firm's success. How to ensure the continued quality of what we provided. Yes, technically I lived in the present, but my eyes were forever focused on a more elusive, seemingly more important spot in time. (Before the diagnosis, my last thought every night before falling asleep usually concerned something that was to happen one month to six months later. After the diagnosis, my last thought before falling asleep was . . . the next day.) In 2002, when I was elected chairman and chief executive officer of KPMG (U.S.), it was for a term of six years. But in 2006, if all went according to plan, I expected I might become chairman of the global organization, probably for a term of four years. In 2010? Retirement, probably.

I was not a man given to hypotheticals—too straight-ahead in my thinking for that—but just for a moment, suppose there had been no death sentence. Wouldn't it be nice still to be planning and building and leading and cage-rattling like I had been, for years to come? Yes and no. Yes, because of course I'd like to have been around for certain things. To see my daughter Gina graduate from high school and college and marry and have children and reinvent the future (in whatever order she ends up doing all that). To spend next Christmas Eve day, the day before my older daughter Marianne's birthday, in last-minute gift shopping with her, eating and talking and laughing the way we did every year on that day. To travel and play golf with my wife of 27 years, Corinne, the girl of my dreams, and to share with her the easeful retirement in Arizona we'd fantasized about and planned for so long. To see my firm, the one I'd been with since before I graduated from business school and had worked at for more than three decades, establish new standards for quality and success. To witness the Yankees win another World Series, or three. To attend the 2008 Olympics in Beijing. To see my grandchildren grow up.

But I also say no. No, because, thanks to my situation, I'd attained a new level of awareness, one I didn't possess the first 53 years of my life. It's just about impossible for me to imagine going back to that other way of thinking, when this new way has enriched me so. I lost something precious, but I also gained something precious.

One day not long ago, I sat atop the world. From this perch I had an overview that was relatively rare in American business, a perspective that allowed me access to the inner workings of many of the world's finest, most suc-

cessful companies, across all industries, and the extraordinary minds that ran them. I could see what was going on
around me. I could make a good guess at how things might
unfold economically over the near future. At times, I felt
like a great eagle on a mountaintop—not because of any
invincibility I felt, but for the overall picture it afforded me.

Overnight, I found myself sitting in a very different
perch: a hard metal chair, looking across a desk at a doctor
whose expression was way too full of empathy for my, or
anyone's, liking.

His eyes told me I would die soon. It was late spring. I
had seen my last autumn in New York.

All the plans I'd made as CEO were shattered—at least,
as far as my seeing them come to pass. While I believed we'd
made great progress on my vision for the firm, someone
else would now have to lead the effort. All the plans that
Corinne and I had made for our future had to be junked.
It was hard not to lament that one of the big reasons we'd
sacrificed so much time together, across so many years, as I
traveled the world and worked ungodly hours—namely,
so that on the other side of it we could enjoy a prosperous
retirement together—had been a tease, only we hadn't
known it. In my wallet I even carried a photo of the dream
spot to which we planned to retire—Stone Canyon, Arizona—but that dream was gone now. Same with all my
other personal goals for 2006, 2007, and every year after that.

I'd always been a goal-driven person. So was Corinne. Throughout our lives together, we'd figured out our long-term goals, then worked backward from there. That is, we structured short-term goals to give us the best chance of meeting the big ones down the road. Any time the situation changed—which was all the time—we re-evaluated our goals, both short and long, and made adjustments so we had the greatest possibility of a good overall result. The goals I'd had the week before the doctor stared at me in that unfortunate way were no longer achievable by me. The quicker I scrapped plans for a life that no longer existed, the better.

I needed to come up with new goals. Fast.

A capacity to confront reality had served me well throughout life. I remember doing so 40 years before, on a much smaller scale, but one that still felt profound. Growing up in Bayside, Queens, a middle-class bedroom community within the confines of New York City but seemingly not of it, I adored baseball. I played all the time. I pitched for my high school team. I thought I was pretty good. I even got written up in the local paper once for getting our team out of a bases-loaded, no-out jam in the last inning to preserve the victory. I thought I might be able to go further.

One day when I was 14, my mother, who for years had witnessed my passion for the sport, told me it was important to distinguish that from talent.

"What do you mean?" I asked.

"You may have the passion to be a great baseball player," she said, "but not the talent."

It took me the better part of that summer to adjust to what my mother had, lovingly, told me. She wanted me to hold onto my passion while also following a path where my talent could flower. I didn't stop playing ball, or being a fan, and I eventually came to see she was right. Freshman year at Penn State, I tried to win a spot on the team as a walk-on but I didn't make it. I didn't have as much talent as my brother, and even he wasn't good enough to get past a certain level.

Like it or not, that was my reality. I adjusted. As I got older, I learned to adjust faster. I cultivated an ability to make big shifts quickly, almost instantly. When something in my life no longer worked, I could abandon it with little senti-ment. I did not look back, nor did I digress from my new path. It seemed to me that no good came from pretending that what used to be true was still true when clearly it wasn't, or that what really was true, no matter how unpleas-ant, really wasn't. The quicker one got on with it, the bet-ter. It was a particularly useful skill in business, a world at least as fast-moving and unforgiving as the larger world.

Within a very few days of that dark moment at the doc-tor's, I acknowledged my timeline was no longer like most people's. *This is the way it is now*, I admitted to myself. Now

I needed to come up with goals that were achievable within that timeline.

Fortunately, because I'd pursued a career for which I seemed to have had talent (and ultimately passion, as well), I could now use my skills and knowledge to take full advantage of this sobering new reality. Instead of figuring out how we as a firm needed to reposition swiftly to adjust to the new circumstances of the marketplace, I would have to figure out how I as an individual needed to reposition swiftly to adjust to the new circumstances of my life. My experience and outlook gave me the potential to manage my endgame better than most, and I considered that opportunity a gift.

The key word in the previous sentence is not *gift* or *opportunity*. It's *potential*. To turn this opportunity into a real gift, one that could never be taken away from me or my family and friends, would be the greatest challenge of my life.

———◦———

This may all seem a little hard to believe. I understand.

After all, who deals with death this way? How can the end *not* get messy—even for an accountant? How can you *not* fall into despair? How can you *not* immerse yourself in denial and an endless, if quixotic, chase for miracles?

Can death really be approached constructively—like every other phase of life? With brightness (if not hope)?

Isn't there an implicit contradiction here? And, perhaps most unbelievable of all, how on Earth can you possibly turn this awful time into the single best period of your life, ever?

For most people, the specter of death is brutally hard to accept. They don't want to spend even a minute thinking about it. They'd rather put it out of their mind, to be thought about—*if* it's thought about—at a later date. Much, much later.

When people met me, however, they could no longer ignore the notion of death—premature, unplanned-for death. I could see it in their eyes. I looked so much older than my 53 years—70 at least, maybe 75. The right side of my face drooped. I looked as if I'd had a stroke, a bad one. Soon my head would be bald from radiation, and the skin on my skull was the texture of tissue paper. (My daughter Gina said I looked like a kindly Dr. Evil, from *Austin Powers*.) My speech was sometimes garbled, as if I were chewing on marbles. One colleague said it sounded like I had suddenly acquired a Massachusetts accent. Now and then it took a few tries for even family members and life-long friends to understand what I was saying. Often I was beseeched to pursue—*please*—some radical course of treatment, in the hope that a miracle might occur. Some friends and colleagues seemed almost offended by my attitude and chosen course, as if I had laid bare the fact that miracles, or their possibility, were ultimately worth rejecting. (Of *course* a part of me hoped that the front page of tomorrow's *New York Times* would announce the miraculous medical breakthrough that would buy me a couple more decades. But I couldn't afford to spend an ounce of energy on that possibility.) Most of the people I met wanted me to live forever—or at least for several more years. That way, the immediacy of what I represented could be made less immediate—to them.

People have written their own eulogies. Certainly they've picked out their cemetery plots and made very clear whether they want to be buried or cremated or to donate their bodies to medical science. But before I came up with the final and most important to-do list of my life, I hadn't known anyone who tried to manage his own death in such a conscious fashion. I did not start out doing it to influence others. I did it simply because that was who I was: methodical, organized, unequivocating, thorough. What can I say? I was an accountant not only by trade, but by manner, as well. The same traits that made me someone who might flourish in the world of finance and accounting also made me someone who did not know how to do anything unplanned—dying included.

I had long believed that a successful businessperson could, if so inclined, live a spiritual life, and that to do so it wasn't necessary to quit the boardroom, chuck it all, and live on an ashram, as if only a physical departure that dramatic would confirm a depth of feeling about larger issues, including one's soul. After my diagnosis, I still believed that. But I also discovered depths to which a businessperson rarely goes, and learned how worthwhile it was to visit there, and sooner rather than later, because it may bring one greater success as a businessperson and as a human being. You can call what I went through a spiritual journey, a journey of the soul. A journey that allowed me to experience what was there all along but had been hidden, thanks to the distractions of the world.

Because I learned so much in my final weeks that seemed remarkable to me (as I suspected I would), I felt the tug to help people see this stage as something worth experiencing *if* you prepare for it. A couple of weeks after my diagnosis, as I strolled through Central Park on a gorgeous day with one of my closest friends, the mentor who had groomed me for my final job, I told him, "Most people don't get this chance. They're either too sick or they have no clue death is about to happen. I have the unique opportunity to plan this about as well as it can be planned." The look he gave me was, I think, more admiration than curiosity, but I can't say for sure.

Back when I was CEO, I expanded our firm's mentoring program so that everyone would have a mentor. Later, as I was dying, I couldn't help but think that learning all I

did about death's approach had forced on me the responsibility to share my experience. I wanted to mentor someone, even one person, with this knowledge I had gained.
Knowledge about winding down relationships. About
enjoying each moment so much that time seems actually
to slow down. About the one thing that's more important
than time (and I don't mean love). About clarity and simplicity. About the death of spontaneity, and the need to
rekindle it in our lives. Weren't these things that healthy
people could learn, or must you have a terminal illness
before the ideas penetrate? Morbid as it sounds, my experience taught me that we should all spend time thinking
about our death, and what we want to do with our final
days, insofar as it's within our control.

I came to wonder, almost marvel, over this question: *if
how we die is one of the most important decisions we can make*
(again, in those situations where it's somewhat within our
control, or, at least, its occurrence is approximately known),
then why do most people abrogate this responsibility? And, in so
doing, sacrifice benefits both for themselves and for the
ones they leave behind? As for those considering taking the
time someday to plan their final weeks and months, three
words of advice: *Move it up.* If you're 50 and you'd planned
to think about it at 55, move it up. If you're 30 and had
planned to think about it in 20 years, move it up. Just as a
person with a terminal illness is motivated to adhere to a

more souped-up schedule, so a person in good health has little motivation to address the situation even one minute before it's time, which may already be too late. That's your disadvantage, maybe even your curse. *Move it up.* A close friend who was invited to participate in a "Renaissance Weekend"—those high-octane gatherings of politicians, artists, academics, captains of industry, Nobel Prize winners, and others—told me that, at the end of the weekend, a select few attendees are asked to give a short speech to everyone assembled. The speechmaker is given no more than three minutes and is instructed to imagine that, as soon as the talk concludes, he or she dies. My friend said that the speeches were uniformly riveting, but, more notably, they were surprising. The men and women charged with the honor of giving these speeches clearly thought hard about what was most essential for them to say, and often it wasn't at all what you might expect from a senator, a world-renowned physicist, or a CFO.

Move it up.

That's not to say I got it completely right. I had lots of work to do. I got a lot of it wrong. When I aimed to be fully conscious and in the moment, I often had trouble keeping my mind from wandering to the future or the past. I got angry. Frequently I cried. Occasionally I got obsessed. I experienced repeated failure at what I was trying to do. But not once did I regret that I had exercised control over my life, the final and most precious inches of my life, for the last real time I was able to.

————◦————

What is wrong with this picture?

I couldn't seriously go into death thinking that my businessman's mindset would now expand to reveal great truths to me, and the world at large, about the profoundest issues we all face, could I? No, I couldn't. That would be arrogance. I was never an overly reflective or philosophical person. While I do believe that the business mindset is, in important ways, useful at the end of life (just as it was useful back when I felt vigorous, indefatigable, and damn near immortal), it sounds pretty weird to try to be CEO of one's own death.

Given the profoundness of dying, and how different its quality felt from the life I led, I had to *undo* at least as many business habits as I tried to maintain. Indeed, though I didn't always have time to reflect on it, it was the struggle between these two poles—the old me and the me that had to be created day by day—that was my biggest challenge, not the dying itself. It was hard to tell myself to be a leader and manager, on the one hand, and, on the other, to release myself once and for all from thinking that way. Which part of me stayed? Which part of me strayed? Which would help me? Which would fail me? Did I become some sort of before-and-after hybrid? Was that a good thing?

An unavoidable thing? Would the right self triumph in the end?

And what might others learn from this tension in my life, and take away for their own benefit?

I tell my story so that those who haven't been given my "gift" may find in here something useful for their future (a long one, I hope) and/or their present (a deep one, I hope). I'll be glad if they come to see the value of confronting their own mortality, and the issues surrounding it, sooner rather than later, and that my approach and perspective might provide help for a better death—and for a better life right now.

Almost exactly 14 years ago, on the day my daughter Gina was born, the nurse placed her in Corinne's arms. I moved closer to my wife and baby girl, awed by what lay before me. My newborn daughter was staggeringly beautiful, if a bit squashed from the journey. Before I could touch her, she reached out, startling me, and grabbed my finger. She held on tightly.

A look of shock darkened my face.

That day and the next I walked around as if in a fog. Corinne picked up on my odd, distracted behavior. Finally, she confronted me.

"What's wrong?" she demanded. "You're acting very strange."

I looked away.

"What is it?" she asked. "Tell me."

I couldn't hide it any longer. "The moment she grabbed my finger," I said, "it hit me that someday I'll have to say good-bye to her."

It's a blessing. It's a curse. It's what you get for saying hello to people. At some point, a good-bye is coming, too. Not just to all the people you love and who love you back, but to the world as well.

I loved being a business leader, but then the day came when I could be that man no more. Before the light in my mind faded and the shadows lengthened too much for me to see anymore, I chose at least, at last, to be master of my farewell.

THE BOTTOM LINE

I INTEND TO LIVE FOREVER. SO FAR, SO GOOD.

—Steven Wright

Who was I?

In my past life, the one where I got to be CEO and chairman of KPMG LLP, the $4 billion, 20,000-employee, century-plus-old partnership, one of America's Big Four accounting firms, here was a Perfect Day: I'd have a couple of face-to-face client meetings, my favorite thing of all. I'd meet with at least one member of my inner team. I'd speak on the phone with partners, in New York and in offices around the country, to see how I could help them. I'd put out some fires. Sometimes I'd have a discussion with one of our competitors about how we could work together toward one of our professional common goals. I'd complete lots of the items listed in my electronic calendar. And I'd move ahead in at least one of the three areas I'd resolved to improve when I was elected to the top spot by the partners of the firm three years earlier: growing our business (hardly surprising, since any business must grow to survive); enhancing quality and reducing risk; and, most vital to me and the long-term health of the firm, making our firm an even better place to work, indeed a great place to work, one that allowed our people to live more balanced lives. I'd long felt that we had to do better at making our employees feel that their jobs and their lives outside of work were extensions of the same organism, not separate, competing entities.

For me personally—for any executive, but especially the top guy—that last plank in the platform was particularly difficult to achieve. Don't get me wrong: I loved my firm. (Part of the struggle may have been because of how much I loved it.) I enjoyed what I did, every day of it—the action, the challenge, the fulfillment. I was passionate about accounting. (Don't laugh.) Its precision, its clarity, its logic. I felt as if I was made for it—my mind, my temperament. I was goal-oriented, felt clear in my mission, was driven to do whatever it took. If you called me in the middle of the night and told me that to win or keep a piece of business

I had to get to the airport right away and fly halfway around the world, I'd do it. In fact, I *did* do it. Back when I was head of the firm's financial services division, its biggest arm, and we were competing to become the auditor for a major investment bank, I knew that if we were really serious about winning the account, I would need to get a face-to-face meeting with the president of the bank's Australian unit. The bank was expected to make its decision very soon. I did everything I could to schedule a meeting with him—made my calendar completely available, called his secretary repeatedly.

Sorry, I was told. His secretary said there wasn't a single moment her boss was in the office that was unbooked. For weeks. If I waited until he had an opening, I knew, the business would be lost.

I called his secretary back. Given how often I'd called her, we'd developed a bit of a rapport. So I figured I'd try: Would she be so kind as to tell me her boss's upcoming travel plans? He was a man on the go, in transit much of the day—surely a pocket of that travel time was not taken up with meetings? She told me that in two days he was flying from Sydney to Melbourne. Nothing was scheduled for the time he was in the air.

"Perfect," I said.

I asked her for his seat assignment. She told me. I called the airline and booked the shortest longest business trip of

my life, reserving the first-class seat next to his. That night
I packed, showered, and shaved, and the following day I
flew the 22 hours from New York to Sydney, landed,
boarded my 90-minute flight bound for Melbourne, sat
down, and introduced myself to the banker I'd flown
halfway around the world to meet, briefly. When I
described what I'd done to get there, he was dumbstruck.
I asked if I could explain why I believed we were the
best firm to audit his bank's books. An hour and a half
later, we touched down. I offered him our presentation,
shook his hand, and headed to another gate for my 20-
plus-hour trek home.

We won the account.

Years later, after I was named chairman and CEO, I felt
as if I had as privileged a position as one can have in
American business. As the accounting firm to giant companies—Citigroup, General Electric, Pfizer, and Motorola,
to name a very few—I got to sit in on their board meetings, where I was lucky enough to be exposed to an array
of some of the most impressive minds in the country. I got
to hear where they thought the global economy was
headed. I came to consider myself a peer—certainly an
admirer—of several chief executives, people like Warren
Buffett, Sandy Weill (Citigroup), Jeff Immelt (GE),
Stan O'Neal (Merrill Lynch), and numerous others. In
the spring of 2005, I was one of 50 CEOs invited to

participate at a White House business roundtable with President Bush.

Was anyone luckier in his job than I?

But the job of CEO, while of course incredibly privileged, was tough. Relentless. Full of pressure. And it was not as if it would ever let up: My calendar was perpetually extended out over the next 18 months. I was always moving at 100 miles an hour. I worked all the time. I worked weekends. I worked late into many nights. I missed virtually every school function for my younger daughter. My annual travel schedule averaged, conservatively, 150,000 miles. For the first 10 years of my marriage, when I was climbing the ladder at KPMG, Corinne and I rarely went on vacation. After that, vacations were mostly rolled into the corporate outings I was required to attend. One year, when we were still living in the Bay Area, our biggest account, based in New York, required my full attention; I lived there for nine months, getting back to the West Coast only on weekends to see my family. Over the course of my last decade with the firm, I did manage to squeeze in workday lunches with my wife.

Twice.

It hadn't always been like that. *I* hadn't always been like that. The summer after my first year of business school, I worked at a Wall Street firm, but I knew I wasn't willing to give my whole life to my job. I wanted balance, always had.

At summer's end, I was offered a job with a top management consultant firm. Corinne and I discussed it. She and
I and Marianne—Corinne's young daughter whom I'd
instantly fallen in love with and adopted to be my daughter—were making our first major decision as a family. If I
accepted the job offer, I'd pretty much be guaranteeing us
big, *big* money down the road—in return for *being* on the
road all the time, working insane hours, spending most of
my life away from my wife and child. Or I could go back
to accounting and the job I'd had at Peat Marwick the previous two years. That would mean less money, less excitement, but more time with my family. More balance in my
life. I'd always aspired to be a Renaissance Man. To know
about wine and opera, to read books. I loved sports and
wanted to be physically active, to spend at least some time
in nature. I considered myself a curious person, and wanted
to learn as much as I could. In short, I did not aspire to
be a CEO.

I returned to being an accountant.

But after a quarter-century at my firm, I rose to the top
position. My life changed. The balance in it faded.
Spontaneity died. Forget stealing away for the midnight
showing of *The Rocky Horror Picture Show*, as Corinne and
Marianne and I once could in San Francisco. Our sub-
scription to the opera frequently went unused. My wine
newsletters sat unread—or, if I did peruse them, I did it

while also doing several other things, the master of multi-tasking. I was always distracted by work. The number of people for whom I was professionally responsible had grown to the thousands. Where once the scale had been mostly work and little play, now it had tipped even further away from balance.

Before this starts to sound like complaining, I must be honest: As long as I believed I could handle such a high-pressure position, I wanted it, and as long as I wanted it, I would never be satisfied with less. As profound as my devotion to and love for my family were, after I'd achieved a certain level of proficiency and accomplishment I could not have settled for a job just because it guaranteed that I would be home each night by six and could make PTA meetings. People don't walk into the top spot. They're driven.

One sanctuary from all the intensity was golf. Golf had been a major and lifelong passion of mine. Seldom, if ever, did I have a bad day on the golf course. I admired what the game called for: honor, personal accountability, precision, mental discipline, and endurance. It required physical ability, too, of course, but anyone who believed talent was the most important club in one's bag did not, in my opinion, understand the game. Once, thanks to the perks of being a CEO, I was fortunate to play a round with PGA star Raymond Floyd, who said the easy part for all the top golfers was getting themselves ready, physically, to succeed at a tournament. The real challenge was training yourself to quiet your mind enough to hit the golf ball well, and to do it shot after shot after shot, day after day, week after week.

I never considered myself good at the game—with a 15 handicap, I thought myself mediocre; on my best day I might be tempted to use the word *proficient*. But my skill was irrelevant. Golf led me to great friendships and experiences (and given how much networking is conducted on and around America's fairways and sand traps and greens, it led to good business, too). Like many executives, I had the privilege to play some of the world's best courses. (After I became chairman, I had far less time to play anywhere.)

But of all the things I loved about golf, the most important was that it allowed Corinne and me to have time to ourselves. In particular, we loved to play late in the day. The course tended to be emptier. The sun was lower in the sky, making the shadows longer and the trees bordering each hole look more impressive and beautiful. It was a magical time to play. When we were out there, we felt almost touched by something, our senses heightened. It was as if we weren't just playing golf, but chasing daylight, grabbing as much time as we could.

In early May of 2005, Corinne and I played golf. My round started well. But on the eighth hole, I teed up the ball, struck it—and it went way right. I don't mean that it sliced; like almost every golfer, I've had my troubles over the years with slicing and hooking. That's not what happened here. The ball went straight, but way, way right from where the hole was, as if I had lined up wrong to begin with, as if I'd had a different target in mind.

The round deteriorated from there. We finished, but afterward Corinne said I looked pale.

I was used to going at breakneck speed. The spring of 2005 was even more frenzied than usual.

Not just for me, but for my family. We'd recently sold our brownstone on the East Side of Manhattan, and Corinne was looking for a new apartment, while dealing with packing and the other details of moving. Gina, finally recovering from a six-month bout with mononucleosis, was finishing a school science project titled "The Blue Rings of Death," in which she computer-modeled the defense mechanisms of the blue-ringed octopus. Not surprisingly, my travel schedule prevented me from attending the science fair. We all knew that if we would just continue to bear down for the next few weeks, until the school year let out, on the other side lay a rare, long-awaited vacation for the three of us—two weeks in Hawaii. (Marianne, who lived a busy life in Napa, had just taken a vacation with her husband and two young children.)

Before I could exhale, though, there was lots for me to do. First, I had to fly to Shanghai to participate in a global economic forum that would include numerous business leaders from around the world. I would also look in on our organization's China practice and spend time with the local KPMG leadership.

On my way to China, I stopped in Fort Worth to meet with Robert Bass of Bass Brothers, a long-time client; then, over the next four days, I flew to Denver, Washington, Montreal, and San Francisco for meetings. While I was in California, our family had gathered for the wedding of my niece. At one point during the rehearsal dinner, Corinne stared at me, oddly, then put her hand to my face.

"There's a droop," she said, touching my right cheek. I didn't feel anything unusual. Later, I noticed it in the mirror only because I knew to look for it. It appeared to me as if I'd come from the dentist and the Novocaine hadn't quite worn off.

There was no panic. Throughout the weekend, Corinne noticed an intermittent tightness around my mouth and the continued sag in the muscles of my right cheek. A few other wedding-goers remarked on it, too, but only after Corinne pointed it out. She assumed it was stress-related, maybe Bell's palsy, which we learned on the Internet was one of the most common neurological disorders; it manifests as facial paralysis, and its cause may be viral. We thought my symptoms might have been triggered by fatigue, in the way one's muscles can start to twitch when one is overworked and exhausted.

Corinne wanted me to go to a doctor, but my China trip loomed. I would address my condition when I returned.

I didn't give it a thought when I was overseas. I didn't have time.

The following week I returned through Seattle for the annual Microsoft CEO Summit, a power-packed affair attended by more than 100 CEOs. Warren Buffett, Berkshire Hathaway's head and probably the world's smartest investor, not only showed off perhaps the driest wit I've ever encountered, but startled me with how much he knew about my world: each opinion he shared on every major accounting issue was incredibly well-informed. Steve Ballmer, Microsoft's CEO, did his usual high-energy presentation.

When I had time to consider the state of my life (*if* I had time), I thought the day-to-day bustle was going extremely well, if supercharged. And Paradise—a.k.a. Hawaii—was not far off.

Back in New York, I still had the drooping muscle in my cheek and at the corner of my mouth, and I agreed to have a neurologist look at it the following week.

The weekend before the appointment with the doctor, Corinne and I entertained a long-time client and his wife,

whom we'd come to consider friends. Over dinner I
recounted excitedly what I'd seen on my business trip, and
the four of us talked about China and India and their growing importance in the world economy. After dinner, we
headed over to Madison Square Garden, where we had
tickets for the U2 concert. It was the loudest event any of
us had ever experienced. Four songs into the show,
Corinne rose from her seat. Bolted, is more accurate.

"What is it?" I yelled to her, trying to be heard above
the noise.

"I feel like our world is about to blow apart," she yelled
back.

I assumed she was referring to the decibel level.

Outside in the corridor, where we could actually hear
each other, she said she'd been trying hard to concentrate
on Bono and the happenings onstage but she simply
couldn't focus. She was overwhelmed by foreboding and
anxiety. She suddenly felt as if our life as we knew it was
about to disintegrate. She said she felt she had no choice
but to move; she rose from her seat as if it was beyond her
control. Nothing like it had ever happened to her before,
she said.

It wasn't the first time in our marriage that she'd picked
up a signal that I'd tuned out.

I assured her that our life was not coming apart. We
returned to our friends and to Bono. The stress in my life

was at such a distracting level, I didn't realize just how insufficiently I had reassured Corinne.

Not that I could have anyway.

━━━━◆━━━━

When Corinne and I showed up at the neurologist's office at Cornell Medical Center on Tuesday, May 24, we were both convinced I was suffering from something stress-related, probably Bell's palsy. It wasn't exactly wishful thinking. After all, my work was routinely stressful, and it had been even more so the previous months and weeks. I'd been doing more than the usual globe-trotting. Our living situation was in upheaval—in between homes now, we'd been staying for the past several days in a midtown hotel. It wasn't hard to imagine that the pressure had finally gotten to me, much as I'd always thrived on it.

The appointment was in the late afternoon, so it wouldn't interfere excessively with my schedule. As I made my way over to the neurologist's office, I couldn't help but think how great it would be to be out on the golf course right now, this in-between time of day, the flat light we'd find there, the serenity. I smiled to think that in just a few weeks I'd be out there. Corinne, Gina, and me in Hawaii. Whatever work stresses I'd been dealing with would be, at least briefly, calmed.

In the neurologist's office, I was asked some questions, then put through what seemed a pretty standard physical exam. The doctor tapped my knee for reflexes, looked into my eyes, tested the strength of my right arm versus my left, and asked me to walk a straight line.

She said she wanted me to come in for an MRI first thing the following morning.

As a businessman, I naturally prized efficiency and promptness. This was one time where the virtue of promptness did not gratify me. I knew that getting bumped to the head of the MRI line was not the sort of privilege you want to experience. If the doctor had really thought the droop of my cheek and the right side of my face had been caused by Bell's palsy or something of that middling severity, then confirming the diagnosis probably could have taken a normal, more leisurely course, with me waiting in line just like everyone else. A week or more.

When a doctor tells you at 5:30 on a Tuesday afternoon that she's scheduling you for an MRI at 8 the next morning, you start to think it could be something worse. Far worse.

I didn't let my mind wander there for long, though, and neither, I thought, did Corinne. When we discussed it that evening, she said she thought the doctor probably just needed to rule out some things, to be sure.

The next morning I went in for the MRI, then headed to the office for a particularly important board meeting. A few hours later, the neurologist called my office. My secretary, Caryn, passed the message on to Corinne, who called the doctor back. The doctor was hesitant to share the results with anyone but me. Corinne persuaded the doctor.

"We found something," the doctor said. The something was in the brain. She wanted to do a second MRI, this one using contrast dye to allow for a better look.

The next day, Corinne and I went in for my second MRI. Had we been going on a normal outing, I would have peppered Corinne with a million questions about what she thought we were in for. I never liked surprises. I always wanted to understand what I was embarking on.

But on the way to the doctor's office, I asked nothing.

After the MRI, I returned to work.

That night, the doctor called. She wanted me to come in the following day so that she could explain the results. I had an extremely busy day ahead of me, including board meetings. Couldn't it please wait until the day after . . .?

"No," said the doctor. She did not advise postponing. Even one day.

The next day, Corinne and I sat in the neurologist's office. She slid the films of the MRIs of my brain onto the light board. Before she said a thing or even gave a name to what we were looking at, the first thought that came to me was: Star Wars.

Compared to the unblemished right side of my brain, the left side looked milky, with dots of varying sizes scattered all over the place. It looked like space. The dots were connected by lines—some sharp, some vague, but there were so, so many of them. As an accountant, I was trained to look at what was before me and, from that, to formulate a plan of attack, an organized, methodical, clear plan. Looking at the MRIs, I couldn't even conceive of how a doctor, no matter how brilliant, might formulate a way to begin confronting the constellation of wispy matter all over the place. Where did it start? Where did it end? Everywhere were thick galaxies.

Star Wars.

Corinne would later say that it looked to her as if the Loch Ness Monster was undulating through the left side of my brain.

The neurologist said she could not yet diagnose what I had with certainty, but she suspected that it was an astrocytoma or glioblastoma; my glial cells, of which the brain has over a trillion, were malignant. There were multicentric tumors, three of them, each the size of— what else?—a golf ball. The tumors were connected and spaced democratically—one each in the frontal cortex (which controls emotions and decision making), the motor cortex in the middle, and the visual cortex in the back.

Then and there the doctor scheduled for us to meet the following day with two of the country's best neurosurgeons. She was so encouraging, we almost believed it wasn't going to be that bad.

I don't think shock had set in just yet. Back at our hotel that night, Corinne said she felt as if, for the first time in our married lives, we'd been caught completely off-guard. We prided ourselves on our teamwork, our ability to anticipate, to take the measure of oncoming predicaments and deal with them, minimizing damage and making the best of things. By complementing each other, by having our ear to the ground in the way each of us was good at, we'd been able to build a good life together and steer clear of disaster.

Not this time.

"Everything we'd planned for our life is not going to happen," Corinne said, deeply upset.

She took a breath. During a crisis, she was at her coolest.

"I don't want to look back someday," she said, "and regret that we wasted even one moment."

Not infrequently over the course of our marriage we'd talked about how each of us—or anyone, for that matter— needed to develop the inner strength necessary to face his or her own death. Not to pay lip service to the concept but really attempt to work at it. People neglected to do so at their peril.

"I think you'd better start working on it," Corinne said later, in a quiet moment. "This is coming up for you. It's not as if you were given a whole phase of life to prepare."

She was only saying what I was thinking. "I don't want to prepare *too* quickly," I said. "The angels might say, 'Oh, *he* looks ready,' and take me early."

My days as a man at the top of his game, vigorous and productive, were done, just like that.

Wow.

Is there any way, really, to prepare for the suddenness? To have that tucked-away fear that lives constantly in all of us—that a calamity can happen, technically, at any moment—be transformed, within days or moments, into reality? To have that fear that you can bury at least sometimes, even most of the time, explode into a new state of being that you can't deny for even a second?

It was beyond jarring. No time frame was given, yet. But it appeared as if I'd been catapulted into the last phase of my life, the one where I was supposed to be wise—wise for my daughters, my grandchildren, those younger than me. Except I'd missed a key stretch of life and still had a lot to learn.

But that was where I was. And if I was going to be of any use to my daughters, especially to Gina, and to my friends and colleagues, and to Corinne, whose preternatural wisdom I'd relied on for so long, I had better get used to where I was, fast.

The next day we met with the neurosurgeons. The first one recommended immediate brain surgery, called "debulking," to reduce the size of the largest tumor and relieve some pressure on the brain (though I felt no pain). He couldn't say if it would give me "more time"; as I said, we'd yet to discuss how much time I had left to begin with. At that moment, I didn't want to know. It would take a month, he said, to recover from the surgery. Radiation could begin sometime after that.

Dire as it was, his evaluation wasn't the part that most scared me.

It was the look of compassion he gave me and Corinne. The look obviously came from the depth of his being. It was an unfortunate kind of intimacy to see in a doctor.

That was the moment, more than any other, when the size of what was happening started to hit me. On top of my shock—which I probably didn't realize I was in the midst of, and would be for at least a few more days—was a creeping sense that this was really happening. To me.

In the afternoon, as Corinne and I sat in the waiting room of our second world-class neurosurgeon of the day, my mind started to reel. I turned to her and said the first thing that came.

"I'm sorry."

She looked at me. She was in shock, too. No words were necessary from her. Probably none had been necessary from me. It had always been like that between us, from the moment we met. From the beginning she had been my one true confidante. And 30 years later, that's where our communion still lay. No elaboration was required.

The second neurosurgeon, a young man who specialized in brain mapping, suggested a more conservative route. "Debulking is brain surgery," he said. "It's at least a month recovery time." Instead, he suggested taking a biopsy of the tumor. The procedure would take about two hours, he estimated.

Something about him—his youthfulness, his conservative approach, a forthrightness I understood—made me hopeful, even if I had no reason to be.

Marianne flew in from California. Gina, who was scheduled to fly to Kentucky for an international school competition on strategic thinking, really did not want to go, but I asked her to. For me, but really for her. I knew what an important opportunity this was, a chance for her to use and exhibit her remarkable ability; such opportunities, I felt, didn't necessarily come around so easily again. She was torn, but I kept asking her please to go. I practically begged her.

She went. She would call repeatedly to ask about me.

On Wednesday, June 1, the biopsy that was supposed to take two hours took three. Halfway through, the surgeon came out to the waiting room (I would learn later) to tell Corinne that the first tissue sample he'd removed from my brain was "necrotic"—dead. Not dying, but already dead.

The tumors, he would say afterward, were inoperable.

It's an understatement to say that it wasn't looking good.

While I lay in post-op, Corinne asked the brain surgeon about our upcoming Hawaiian vacation. "If you go on the trip," he told her, "he will not make it back."

Later, when I'd recovered from the procedure and the doctor could address Corinne and me together, he said he recommended radiation, which might provide a couple of extra months more than whatever I had left. There was no cure for this, he said. "This is terminal. It's not as if you can come back from it."

We asked about chemotherapy.

"Chemotherapy could buy some time," he said. Chemotherapy has a role, often a huge one, to play in the lives of people with certain cancers, cancers from which one could recover. But this was not such a case. Still, despite that, he (along with other doctors) pushed my under-going chemo. It might grant me some more time— as might radiation—if either succeeded in reducing the three golf-ball-sized tumors. But those with my disease— glioblastoma multiforme, it was called—who were most likely to benefit from chemo were those diagnosed early. They were the ones with a decent shot to make it as long as eighteen months. The majority (about 80 percent) would get around six months. It wasn't really a bell-shaped curve.

But I wasn't even in that *second* group, really. I'd be lucky to get three months, even with treatment that worked. My vision was already starting to blur. I wasn't sure when I had first become symptomatic; Corinne and I thought hard about it but couldn't really come up with earlier signs. Caryn, my assistant, pointed out that I'd had a few headaches in the previous months—not severe ones, and they subsided after an aspirin, but I'd never really had headaches before, ever. I was not one of those who had been diagnosed early. Perhaps it was because I had always had my foot to the pedal, never stopping to look up.

The doctors all agreed that there was one piece of good news: Not only was there no pain now (something I could verify), but they predicted that there would be none throughout, even at the very end. I would most likely slip peacefully into a coma.

A week before, I was living my life. Now I was contemplating my death.

With the biopsy behind me, Corinne and I returned to the first surgeon, the one who'd recommended immediate brain surgery, the more radical approach. We wanted to update him on my condition, ask if he had any new ideas, see if he still recommended debulking. After looking at my most recent set of films, he said, "It's so far advanced, it's past the point where we can do even that."

The disease had its own foot to the pedal. Like me, it didn't know how to slow down.

The Business of
Dying Is Hard

———

If we take care of the moments, the years will
take care of themselves.

—Maria Edgeworth

At home, Gina seemed to orbit around me, unsure of
how to be. That shouldn't have been surprising: she
was 13, and her usually healthy and active father had his
head stapled shut from the biopsy. But her big sister
Marianne—twice a mother, someone more experienced
in the messiness of life—showed the way. When she saw
me, she immediately threw her arms around me, which
probably enabled Gina to follow suit and become a little
more comfortable with what was going on—disease,
wounds, uncertainty.

When it was just the four of us in the new apartment during those surreal first few days and nights, a familiar rhythm took hold, which provided some comfort. We all supported each other. Marianne and Gina spent lots of time together, watching movies and talking. All our sleep patterns were screwed up. Each of us would collapse from exhaustion at a different part of the evening. Gina and I would often find ourselves up in the middle of the night. She could hear me crying. I might climb into bed with her. I might go to the desk to write my first notes for what would become this book, and she would just come and sit with me. She might read poetry to me. I'd always given her books of poetry, including one I had had as a child, but I never had a gift for understanding it. I was not wired for poetry. She was. She wrote it and read it. I'd always thought she had in her the best of her mother and me. Yet it amazed me that someone who had come from me and the person I knew best in the world—Corinne—might be a human being I could have never even imagined.

One night, she pulled out "Death, Be Not Proud" by John Donne.

DEATH, BE NOT PROUD, THOUGH SOME HAVE CALLED THEE
MIGHTY AND DREADFUL, FOR THOU ART NOT SO

The poem compared death to an eternal sleep. I didn't agree with the poet's idea. To see death as sleep was contrary to my feeling—a hope but also a belief—that whatever comes next has more consciousness to it than sleep.

It was around one in the morning. At this point, I was not making judgments. I was simply eager to gather different viewpoints.

Probably it goes without saying: I'd never had to make a psychological shift on this scale. Nothing I'd gone through before this was even close. When I was 14 and my mother told me it was important to separate passion from talent—wanting to shield me from the pain of spending all my time at baseball, a pursuit I clearly didn't have the ability to succeed at past the high school level—it was a blow, but I adjusted. Still, it took me the better part of the summer of 1966 to adjust to my new reality.

Now, I didn't have a summer to adjust. I barely had a summer, period. I would need to make the quickest, most dramatic costume change of my life. If I was going to emerge from the misery of my condition and somehow make something positive from it, I would have to do it fast and efficiently—and get it right the first time.

In short, I would have to think the way I'd always thought, plan the way I'd always planned, be the person

I'd always been—an accountant, a business executive, a CEO.

In the moments immediately following a business loss—after learning, say, that we'd lost a potential engagement to a competitor—I would ask several questions of my team and myself:

What caused them to not choose us? What caused them to choose the other guys? Did we do everything we could? Honestly? Was there any lack of commitment? If we had to do it again, would we have done anything differently? What?

I didn't pose these questions to my team with hostility, but with encouragement. So long as we'd done all we could, we could keep our heads high. So long as we answered these questions honestly, we could feel confident that next time we would be better prepared. The postmortem was over pretty quickly. It was time to move forward, to have our eyes on the next opportunity.

Now, with my diagnosis, I was going to have to figure out both the biggest questions and their answers quickly, thoughtfully, correctly.

Corinne had been right: the life we'd known and enjoyed and built together was utterly blown apart.

Together, over the years, we had chased daylight. And now, as a team, we were going to chase it one last time, only when the daylight faded this time, it would fade not just on one beautiful day among many, but on our beautiful life together. Shadows would lengthen for the last time. Night would fall for the last time. At some point, she would have to finish her round without me.

———◆———

I'd never personally known anyone who was struck by glioblastoma multiforme. Also called a Grade IV astrocytoma, it was the most common and aggressive of the primary brain tumors. It was highly malignant, infiltrated the brain extensively, and sometimes became enormous before symptoms appeared, which could include headaches, seizures, vision problems, motor problems, cognitive problems, memory problems, and personality changes. Its cause remains unknown.

I'd never once been close to my own death before, at least not for more than a split second. In my thirties, while in Milan for business, I had stepped off the curb of a traffic circle, unaware that cars were coming from a second direction, one I hadn't checked for . . . and a speeding bus missed me by inches. It terrified and unnerved me for a moment, and obviously the instant stayed with me. But it didn't exactly have me reexamining my life priorities.

But now . . . what would I do now? What would our life be like from now on? I would need to recalibrate in every way.

I knew hope existed, and I knew it was largely up to me to uncover it. I remembered when my good friend Bill had had a seven-way heart bypass. After three days of lying in his hospital bed, he was told by the doctor that he could take 25 steps. Bill did his exercise in the morning, then asked if he could take 25 more steps later that day. Soon, he was shuffling down the hall four times a day. On one of his outings, he peeked into another room, where a couple of fellow heart patients lay quietly, IVs in their arms. "Wow, they have it a lot worse than me," he said to the nurse. "No, actually you have it a lot worse than they do," she said. "They perceive themselves as heart attack victims. You're trying to get better."

That was the kind of spirit I needed. But first I needed another spirit.

On Sunday, Corinne and I walked to our church, St. James, on Madison Avenue and 71st Street. Over the years we'd frequently gone there to pray, though not as much as I would have had my schedule allowed. It gave me a needed sense of tranquility to be there. Sometimes, if I had a difficult work decision to wrestle with, I would go to church, and it was as much for the serenity of the chapel and the moment, which made it easier for me to find objectivity, as for any hope of divine intervention; to function well as a leader, I now and then needed peace and quiet to find the right answer. I couldn't afford to make decisions always on the move, where those decisions might be motivated by anger or fear or impatience. Of course, at times I felt a particular pull to go to church for my family—for instance, the time Gina, in first grade, was suffering from juvenile arthritis, requiring her to be on crutches for six months. You could find me in church often that year. More recently, Corinne and I would go when not a lot of people were there. Saturday was a favorite. We'd sit in the chapel silently, side by side, then go for lunch and share our impressions.

I felt as if I had learned how to pray only when I became an adult. As a child, I'd been taught to pray—I went to Catholic school through ninth grade and had been an altar boy—but I hadn't made a strong connection with it. Not until I got older had I ever felt a *need* to pray.

On that day in early June, I needed to pray, to be in a house of worship, more than I could ever remember.

In the discombobulating few days since the diagnosis, one thought that had not crossed my mind was "Why me?" As terrible a couple of weeks as I was having, my life to that point had been touched by such good fortune, and so many other people around the world had dealt with so many worse things, that it didn't occur to me that I'd been dealt a low blow, or that there was some reason, cosmic or otherwise, that had caused me in particular, among my circle of family and friends and acquaintances, or me in particular, among people in my privileged professional position, or me in particular, among 53-year-old Irish-American males, to be struck by inoperable, late-stage brain cancer. There had been no history of brain cancer in my family. I'd always enjoyed excellent health. In fact, I'd hardly ever been sick in my life. I ran, played golf and tennis, never smoked, ate well, woke at 5:30 every morning, and got to bed at 11 every night. Some things just can't be explained.

But I admit I was a bit rattled when Corinne and I sat down in the pew at St. James that Sunday and our reverend stood behind the podium to begin that week's gospel, the gospel that virtually every Christian church around the world was hearing on that particular Sunday. Luke, Chapter 18.

Jesus and the Tax Collector.

Corinne and I looked at each other.

"Two men went up into the temple to pray; one was a Pharisee, and the other was a tax collector," the reverend read from the New Testament. "The Pharisee stood and prayed to himself like this: 'God, I thank you, that I am not like the rest of men, extortioners, unrighteous, adulterers, or even like this tax collector. I fast twice a week. I give tithes of all that I get.' But the tax collector, standing far away, wouldn't even lift up his eyes to heaven, but beat his breast, saying, 'God, be merciful to me, a sinner!'"

I couldn't help but get a chill, even a bitter smile, that of all the gospels, the liturgical calendar should have offered up this one.

"For it is easier for a camel to enter in through a needle's eye," read the reverend, "than for a rich man to enter into the Kingdom of God."

How could I make things work again? Or let me rephrase that: since they were never again going to work the way they had, how could I make things work?

Would the skills and optimism that had served me so well as CEO (e.g., the ability to recover quickly after losing a piece of business, so that the firm and the team could taste success again, and quickly) serve me now? Were the words I had so often used to exhort colleagues and employees empty ones, now that the challenge before me was of such magnitude? Or could I walk the walk—and by adhering to those principles I had espoused and lived by, make them seem even more enduring?

I'd always preached commitment to goals: setting them, pursuing them, completing them. Now that we'd completed our fact-finding with doctors, I resolved to do three things:

1. leave my job and

2. choose a medical protocol that allowed me to . . .

3. make the time remaining the best of my life, and as good as it could possibly be for those most affected by my situation.

While I made the decisions quickly, it was even more important that the decisions be utterly clear, to both me and others. I had to commit to them. I imagined that other people in my situation had often known the right course to take but were fearful of sticking with their plan. I don't mean to sound as if they were weak and I was strong; I just knew that it was in my best interest to continue to live by the rules I'd followed in my business life. There, clarity of mission, commitment, and execution had always been critical.

Immediately, my energy and focus changed from the priorities I had set for my firm to new priorities I would set for the months remaining to me. As head guy, I had focused on building and planning for the future. Now, I would have to learn the true value of the present.

On June 8, two weeks after I'd gone in for my first, still-innocent-seeming medical test, I told my fellow partners at KPMG that I was stepping down as chairman and CEO. Because of my health situation, I was moving on to the next phase of my life. I said I would involve myself in the management transition, but then I would be gone. I did not use the word *temporary* or *hiatus*. I left no door open. I was done. To say otherwise would have been unfair to the firm and the new chairman, as well as our employees; they deserved certainty of leadership. I hoped and expected that my successor would continue pursuing the initiatives I'd begun, which I felt were improving the organization. But direction and style, and the mandate itself, would be someone else's now, not mine.

Anyway, if I was really going to be honest about my situation, I had to acknowledge that any suggestion that I might return one day would be incredible self-delusion: I was already showing more symptoms.

Did the resignation hurt? Of course. Work defined me as much as anything. I'd been with the firm for 33 years. I'd never known another place. When I first started there, it was less than half its current size, and the sun had just set on the era when the partners were required to wear suits and fedoras when calling on clients. Now, there were 20,000 employees.

But to be faithful to everything I believed, and to what lay ahead, I had to leave, leave now, and leave without remaining, even vaguely, in the shadows.

As soon as the news of my resignation ran on the wire services, I received countless notes and calls, all heartwarming. Many friends from the business world contacted me or my office to express their support, sadness, and shock. My counterpart at another of the Big Four firms was particularly generous in his response. I know this kind of reaching out might happen in other industries, but our profession is notable for its collegiality. During this horrible period, in which the world I knew had splintered so suddenly, it was especially gratifying to know that a certain harmony, especially in business, continued to exist.

My transition from leader of the firm to a former member was swift, as I wanted it. (I did remain a senior partner.) All those scheduled meetings and obligations on my notoriously extended calendar—those for the next few weeks and those six months down the road—were cancelled, reassigned to others within the firm, or would soon be assumed by the new chairman. I was involved in the search for, and transition to, a new leader. It would take roughly three days. My dealings were almost exclusively by phone, from home.

It was on the second day, while talking on the phone with a board member, that I had the first seizure.

———⋄———

It was actually kind of funny.

The seizure was small—"focal," it's called, because the wave of electrical impulses firing through me did not involve the whole brain (as it does in a "grand mal" seizure), but rather a more limited area, a neural network. The muscles on the right side of my face began to spasm.

It happened while I was in bed, on the phone, consulting with a board member about the transition. What made it funny? It was all I could do to hold the wildly twitching side of my face still so I could be understood.

The whole thing lasted a half-hour. Later, we called the doctor, who adjusted the medication. Three days later I had another focal seizure that caused twitching, and again the medication was increased. Not all the seizures involved the motor cortex, which can cause muscles to twitch. Some involved the visual or frontal cortex. Fortunately, my seizures weren't yet grand mal, the kind where you fall to the floor and jerk uncontrollably. Often, I closed my eyes to control the onset of a seizure in the visual cortex. Corinne said that when I did this, I wore a blank expression, and it seemed as if I was looking through her, as if my mind could not be reached.

The seizure was not my first symptom, though.

My eyesight was the first thing to be noticeably affected; one of the tumors was pressing on the visual cortex. Within days of the diagnosis I suffered major vision loss. Blurriness. I couldn't see well enough to write a check. Blind spots appeared about a third of the way out from my field of vision, and were especially pronounced on my right side. I had no trouble seeing what was directly in front of me, but when I walked down the street, I preferred my companion to be on my right, to reduce the chance I might bump into a signpost. And because I often kept my eyes partly closed, I had to be extra careful. Walking up and down stairs, I began to put my hands out, for balance.

Although I remained mostly lucid, now and then I would become a bit confused. I had to relearn how to dress. I needed to do it in an orderly, methodical fashion. I was like a little kid: my clothes were arranged for me. Corinne would lay my shirt on the bed, button-side down, so when I picked it up, I could put it on just the way I was holding it, and the shirtfront would appear where it was supposed to be, not turned around. (Corinne packed away all my shirts with French cuffs; they were way too difficult.) Eventually it would become easier, but getting something over my head was a chore. Even when I was able to do it, the effort exhausted me. Once, I caught Gina standing in the doorway, watching me struggle to maneuver a sweater over my head. I didn't know which of us considered the spectacle more painful. I knew she had always seen her dad as competent, someone who performed at a high level, quickly, efficiently.

He still saw himself that way, most of the time.

For the first time since I was a child, I had to think about basic movements. I became more aware of things that, if you are going to do them at all, you simply can't be aware of. I had to be my old systematic self, but now merely to complete incredibly basic tasks. When writing correspondence, I'd suddenly be confronted by a word I knew but couldn't spell or pronounce. It wasn't the cognitive part of the thought that got me; it was something else, something I couldn't explain. For example, if you asked me to spell *misapplication,* I obviously knew how to do it . . . yet I might not be able to. Why?

My speech became even more garbled.

We went to see a great doctor, a legend in his seventies known as the "grandfather of neuro-oncology." He mostly taught now, but occasionally saw patients. I asked him the big question:

How much time?

"You're not a statistic," he said. "The median is a year from the point of diagnosis." I understood, and knew that Corinne did too, that that "one year" figure was probably too generous in my case. Some people would have been symptomatic earlier and thus diagnosed earlier.

That night, as Corinne and I tried again to piece together my behavior and bearing in the weeks and months leading up to my facial paralysis, we realized I'd been unusually tired for quite a while, but at the time neither of us had thought it extraordinary. She remembered a big bruise on my leg around the time of my niece's wedding, a bruise I'd gotten from having bumped into a car in a parking lot—just walked right into it. At least now I had a legitimate excuse for why my golf game had been off for some time.

Doing our own math, it seemed as if I had three to six months, depending.

The trouble I had getting dressed—doing anything in sequence—began to affect other activities. One night, while watching a Yankee game, I saw an amazing outfield throw and play at the plate, and wanted to share it with a friend, a fellow baseball fan. I dialed his number and, on speakerphone, began to recount the moment. When, after a minute, he failed to share my excitement, I suspected something was amiss. I looked down at the phone. I hit the "Speaker" button, which I'd neglected to do at the start of the call.

"Hello?" I said.

"Hello, Gene," said my friend. He knew I was somewhere out there, he said, and just waited until I figured it out.

"Did you hear any of what I said about the play at home?"

"No," he said. "You'll have to repeat it."

———————

I had resigned as chairman. Task 1 accomplished. The firm, its leaders, and all our people handled the transition beautifully. It made me even more proud of my firm—my second family—that this could be done so smoothly, with no loss of confidence from any corner.

Now I had to address Task 2: settle on a medical protocol.

Chemotherapy, I understood, was not that protocol. Chemotherapy, as the doctors had told me, is at the core of many, if not most, cancer-fighting treatments; it's very often the way you survive cancer. And the protocol for treating my particular type of cancer included chemotherapy, too—but not to offer a chance for survival. After consulting with a top collection of a neurologist, two neurosurgeons and an oncologist, I was satisfied that they had got it right: I would not survive my illness. So in my case, the chemo might prolong my life by two or three months—*might*—though no one was making promises. And for all that uncertainty, the drugs would have toxic effects on my body, curtailing my ability to enjoy life. Ergo, chemotherapy would not save my life, *plus* it would undermine my basic goal.

Why, then, did I take it even once?

Because I had to turn over that stone, examine it, and then be comfortable with my decision—my *own* decision. I wasn't willing to take someone else's word. When making a particularly important business decision, I insisted I had all the facts so that I could judge for myself. Nothing different here.

I quit chemo after three days. That's how long it took for the chemicals to begin affecting me—or *seem* to be affecting me, which is pretty much the same thing. The chemicals interfered with my bodily functions, my normal physical systems. I could feel it in my kidneys and in my liver. I felt nausea. I felt more vulnerable to infection and other illness. Plus, chemo was interfering with something else that was very important: my being able to visualize the radiation (which I'd also begun) actually shrinking the tumors.

"I'm being distracted by my liver and kidneys," I told Corinne. "I can't focus on my brain tumor."

As much as, and maybe more than, the physical wear of chemo's well-documented and invasive side effects was the psychological burden. As soon as I (or anyone) started chemo, a great deal of control was relinquished. I had turned myself over to drugs. Drugs would now run my life. Drugs would determine my daily routine. What's more, once I had started chemo, my focus was no longer on the cancer—and even less so on my life outside the cancer— but instead on other issues that hadn't been issues before (like kidney function). The accountant in me did not like to be distracted from the most important tasks, the tasks I really needed to think about. The manager in me, the one who believed in tight control, abhorred my suddenly letting myself become a person managed by a drug schedule, not my own schedule. I particularly didn't like how, on so much medication, particularly steroids, my moods were no longer mine to manage.

I understand that, to fix a problem, one sometimes needs to take what seems a temporary backward step—in business, it's referred to as reorganization—but here it didn't seem warranted to add many other, avoidable problems to my one huge problem.

In short, I was poisoning myself. Why? The end result would be the same, if slightly longer in actual hours or weeks. Was it really worth wearing myself out—not to mention wearing out my loved ones and/or those who would be helping to care for me at the end—just to extend a diminishing life by a short period of time? Especially when what remained of that life would certainly be more complicated, less rich, less energetic—*less full of life*—because I was poisoning myself?

I resolved that I would make up in quality what I lacked in longevity.

Once I quit chemo, my mission felt much clearer to me—and, not inconsequentially, to those around me. Side effects would no longer be an issue. (And anyway, there's really nothing very "side" about them, when symptoms like kidney pain can seemingly dominate your life even more than the cancer.) I understood and sympathized with how other people in my situation (maybe most people in my situation) would want to grab at any possibility, no matter how remote or even unsubstantiated, to prolong their life. I can understand how someone not experiencing such a threat to his or her life might view my quick abandonment of chemo a form of surrender, as if I really didn't want to extend my life.

I didn't see it that way. I loved my life. I wanted to live as long as I could. I'd now made watching the sun rise on 2006, improbable as it was, my goal.

Stopping chemo didn't just make me feel comfortable. It made me feel liberated. It made me feel great.

Even more than resigning from my job, I felt as if *this* was my first real decision in taking control of my death. To be honest, though, once I'd decided to make this last stage of my life the best stage, and to opt for the highest quality of life at every turn, the decision to forego chemotherapy wasn't just an easy decision. It was no decision at all.

Although chemotherapy was out, I stuck with the radiation. There was a decent chance, according to the oncologist (he refused to give statistics for survival), that radiation could shrink the tumors and relieve the symptoms caused by the growing tumors and the swelling of surrounding tissues, thus providing me with more time—clear-headed, clear-eyed time—to complete the several things I needed to do before I died. It would also give me an important mental boost knowing that each workday for the six weeks of treatment, I was concretely, unambiguously doing *something* to slow the tumor growth, to fight it. (You're making a fight of it with chemo, too, of course, but you're also fighting yourself, essentially opening the gates to allow the enemy entry. It can be demoralizing to think that it's quite possible you're killing off more good things inside you than bad.) Because radiation didn't make me fuzzy-headed, I felt as if I could focus on the tumors, on stopping their growth. Although radiation would fatigue me, it threatened none of the nastier side effects of chemotherapy. And while having to be someplace five times a week for six weeks obviously limited my mobility, it seemed a trade worth making.

What I didn't count on was that the radiation process—not the radiation itself, but the process and everything that surrounded it—would cause different troubles. And that these troubles would help teach me one of the first, most fundamental lessons of my new life.

Typically, my radiation sessions took place in the late afternoon. Corinne had wisely chosen that time slot because the treatment caused physical fatigue, and this way I would have energy for a good part of the earlier day, until it was time for my session. At night, I would get some energy back, enough to enjoy dinner with the family.

Here's how it worked when I got to the clinic:

I would show up in golf clothes, which I wore to get in a good mood, as if I were going off to play a round. When my turn came, they would place what looked like a fencer's mask, with a waffle-like covering, over my face. It was clamped under my chin; then the whole contraption, with me in it, was screwed into a special table. (It was a good thing that I'd never been claustrophobic.) As secured as I was, I was instructed to try not to move my head even one-eighth of an inch, or else the concentrated, laserlike radiation beams that were aimed and then shot at my head from five computer-aligned angles would not work well. If I moved even a little, the process would take longer; they might have to repeat shooting certain beams. I was warned even against swallowing—which, I would discover, I could refrain from doing for the time required, when everything went according to plan.

Like my disease itself, the radiation was painless. Pinched and invasive as the setup may sound, when my head was in the clamped-in mask and then when the beams were emitted, it didn't hurt. I could feel where the lasers went in, but it wasn't painful; it was hardly even unpleasant. It felt more like a vibration. I imagined my head in a microwave oven—not a place you might volunteer to put your head, but benign.

The shooting of the beams, all five of them, took two to three minutes. The whole process, from loading and locking me into the mask and screwing me onto the table to getting me off it and sending me on my way until the next day, took maybe 20.

That was when everything went according to plan.

Things don't always go according to plan. Often they don't. You'd think my experience in the business world, and in the world in general, would have prepared me for this, but for some reason it did not. You'd think the suddenness of my diagnosis, after a life of good health, would have more recently taught me this. It did not. My forward-looking, optimistic outlook had shielded me from doubt and low expectations. Somehow, I had assumed that hospitals and cancer treatment centers would run smoothly.

I soon found out they didn't work like that. Sometimes people at the clinic, no matter how professional and well-meaning they might be, screwed up. More likely the machines did, about one in three times. When that happened, the day, for me and the other patients, became more complicated.

As I said, I'd never experienced claustrophobia. But if the process took longer than it should have—more than the expected 20 minutes, say—I felt a wave of panic set in. And it wasn't caused by a sense of nearness and pressure so much as by the demands the extra time made on my body. I had trained myself not to swallow for the expected 20 minutes. But when 20 minutes had come and gone, I could start feeling my saliva—and the saliva was winning. It began to interfere with my breathing. Suddenly, a half-hour had elapsed. I felt as if I might soon choke. Forty minutes passed. Still I couldn't move my head.

Some sessions I would show up and one of the intermittently balky machines would already be on the blink. The schedule was backed up, and all of us there would be getting started later. For an already high-stress environment and group—there were usually four to six of us patients waiting in each of the four "modules" in the office—the increase in tension was not welcome. You could feel the upset in the waiting room.

The particular machine into which all my vectors were programmed—"Old Reliable," as Corinne and I liked to call it—was, as our nickname for it suggested, one of the more dependable contraptions. But often a mechanical issue (a stubborn lever not locking into position, for instance) left me on the table too long. Or they needed to take an x-ray.

I was subject to the whims of machinery and the medical system, of human competence and freak good or bad fortune. I kept a score of Man versus Machine. If there was a delay of more than 25 minutes, then the machines had won that day. Still, delays or not, I was one of the luckiest ones there. Some of my fellow cancer patients were considerably younger than I. Many of them, unlike me, were experiencing physical pain, often excruciating pain, from their cancer or from some related issue. They often felt degraded by the whole experience. Some had traveled many hours, on multiple modes of mass transit, to get there and had the same trip back, and had to do it four or five days a week. When their dedicated machine broke, it sometimes seemed as if it might just break them too, break their will. Like me, some of these people were confronting the final stage, trying to wind down their lives, but they were less well equipped to do it, or didn't even know how to get started. One patient, awaiting her radiation, barked and occasionally yelled into her cell phone as she paced the waiting room and tended to the details of selling her business. Many of the other patients in the room looked upset by her raving. When she hung up, she turned to all of us. "I'm so sorry," she said, genuinely.

I nodded. I wasn't upset by her outburst of emotion, or her goal. I understood.

The business of dying is hard. The wrapping up. The paperwork, the legal work. The stuff that's boring and maddening about life when life is going well. Of course, the other stuff that's happening when dying—the physical stuff and the huge emotional stuff—can be unspeakably awful. But if paperwork is enough to break your spirit—and it is—then how can you have anything left? Day by day, observing the medical practitioners and especially the patients, I started to understand.

Just months before, and for my whole life before, I had been used to—and expected—people operating at a very high standard. If they didn't, they might lose my confidence. That's just the way the business world worked. I don't mean to say that I or we lacked all compassion; it's just that our index for evaluating people was competency.

Proficiency. Quality. It had to be. If someone said something that in my opinion was carelessly conceived—
whether it was one of the firm's senior partners or my
teenage daughter—I was not above telling him or her that
it was "a stupid thing to say." I expected the most from
myself, too. I was known to flash a temper.

My daily experience at the radiation clinic made me
realize that proficiency was *not* the index I could always use
anymore. Or even usually use anymore. Not everyone can
perform at the level you'd like. Or that they'd like. They
simply can't, try though they may. Maybe they don't have
the physical energy. Maybe their will is shot. Maybe they're
overwhelmed by what they need to do to make a good
break with life. As difficult as my trip to the clinic should
have been, I felt that each time I went there, my tolerance
for people—that is, my tolerance for imperfection—
expanded. I understood better the range of human capa-
bility; it was far broader than I'd thought. In my previous
life, I'd dealt mostly with people at the top of their game.
Now I was dealing with people whose capabilities had
been diminished. By disease, doubt, fatigue.

Things don't go according to plan.

In fact, they almost never did. Now I realized why it was
that I dressed in golf clothes every day: because I knew that
to have a day go the way you want it to—merely to shoot
par—was a great thing. A perfect thing. No one in that

room was asking for double eagles or holes in one, although they'd happily take a miracle if it presented itself. If everyone in that room simply got to stay on schedule with the machines and nothing screwed up (if we shot par), that was tremendous. Par was good enough. Par was great. Par was amazing.

And if I didn't shoot par? If things didn't go as planned?

That would have to be good, too. There was always something that could make even a bad day or a bad round good. One nice shot. One kind gesture. Something.

Sitting in that room, waiting for my turn to have the waffle-mask put over my face and then screwed into a table so they could zap my brain with laser beams, I was learning to accept. I had to accept. I had no recourse but to accept.

When things didn't go the way those of us there wanted, I watched people around me grow frustrated. I tried not to let it happen to me. I couldn't change what was happening, and neither could they. But they were having a far worse time of it by not accepting.

As I watched others get upset, I saw myself in my past life.

It was at the clinic that I really began to understand acceptance. To accept acceptance, if you will. Having entered the final phase of my life, what choice did I have *but* to accept it? Apparently, I wasn't too old to learn something new. *You can't control everything*, I told myself, as hard as it was to hear myself, a Type A personality, say those words. I wouldn't allow mishaps and bad luck and especially a defeating attitude to throw me off my goals, one of which was to try and make every day the best day of my life. The CEO, the micro-manager, needed finally to let go.

I closed my eyes. I let go.

THE BEST DEATH POSSIBLE

MAY YOU LIVE EVERY DAY OF YOUR LIFE.

—Jonathan Swift

From my dining room table, I could see the majestic United Nations building and, just beyond that, the East River. One end of the table was covered by the stack of family papers that came with ordinary life—bills, magazines and newsletters yet to be read, invitations to parties and charity events. Next to it was a bigger stack, the one that came with extraordinary life—dozens of condolence cards, notes of hope and prayer from friends and colleagues who'd heard. Next to that was another sizable collection: medicine bottles. Keppra to minimize my chance of another seizure. Dexamethasone, a steroid, to reduce swelling in the brain. Antibiotics. In the previous few days, new symptoms had appeared—restlessness (from the steroid) and more trouble sequencing things—but, on the plus side of the ledger, my vision had become less blurred.

Before me was my daughter's Apple laptop, even though I could already feel my ability on the computer eroding. Next to that was a legal pad whose pages I'd begun filling with thoughts for the book I intended to write about how I had embraced death, life's ultimate adventure, and what I learned from it. Though my thinking had not yet been affected by my illness (or so I believed), the same could not be said of my handwriting.

Physically I am strong have no
ailgments & since not doing
chemo not subject to that
slow death experience

As I wrote, I peeked at my watch every few minutes, making sure I was on schedule.

But what schedule? What would happen if, rather than dissipating the energy I was spending on the current activity by always having the next one in mind, I concentrated *completely* on what I was doing at the moment, without a care about what came next? How slow or fast would time elapse if I completely immersed myself in what I was doing?

It would certainly be a novel experience.

I suspected that watch-peeking and constant time management, habits of my former life, would have to stop, or at least be reset to my new reality. If my timeline had changed dramatically, then my approach to time had to change dramatically as well. Had I lived into my late seventies—hardly an outlandish dream just months before, since I'd enjoyed good health all my life until this glaring exception—I would have had about 10,000 days left to me. Instead, I had 1 percent of that: 100. I would compensate for the lost 99 percent with a new mindset—a deeper, less cluttered awareness of each moment.

I just didn't know how the hell I was going to get there.

I had so little time left to learn—yet, ironically, the first (and maybe the last) thing I needed to learn was how to slow down. For years I'd been going 100 miles per hour, all straightaway, no turns. On the day I died, I would be going zero. I had assumed (like most people, probably) that later in life, I would come to some natural bend in the road—retirement, say, or age 65, or a tipping point of physical ailments—and some light would go on and I would understand that this was the signal to start slowing down.

The signal had come all right, but without warning. As Corinne had said to me: "It's not as if you're getting a final phase of life to prepare for death." I was slowing, for sure, but in an unmanaged way, a way that was partly out of my control, yet partly within it. And that was the part I needed to focus on: the part I controlled. Having stepped down from the chairmanship and removed myself from the daily interactions of a person on the go, particularly a New Yorker on the go, I figured I was now driving 50 miles an hour, maybe 40. (Maybe 30.) I wanted the continued downshifting to be done consciously, in a controlled way, so that my final weeks and days, and certainly my final moments, could be full of ease and peace.

I did not want to die in a crash.

———◈———

Sitting at the dining room table, I made a to-do list for my final days.

- ❖ Get legal and financial affairs in order
- ❖ "Unwind" relationships
- ❖ Simplify
- ❖ Live in the moment
- ❖ Create (but also be open to) great moments, "perfect moments"
- ❖ Begin transition to next state
- ❖ Plan funeral

Boiled down, I wanted this last period to be marked by resolution and closure; by heightened awareness; by the pleasure and joy of life. Boiled down still further, I wanted these things, and only these things:

Clarity. Intensity. Perfection.

What more could anyone hope for, really?

There's a great blessing, probably Irish: Here's to a good life and a better death. Well, I wanted the best death possible. I didn't mean it in a competitive way, as in, I'm used to winning, so I'm going to win at this, too; as in, I'm going to have a better death than you are. I meant that I wanted to achieve in death what I'd always tried to achieve in life: to do it the best way I knew how. Over the years, I'd come to love wine, and the way I did that was to taste all kinds and to subscribe to wine newsletters and read them when I could. I came to love and understand opera by seeing it and listening to it, and also by reading the story ahead of time. I didn't want just to dabble.

Now, I was motivated to "succeed" at death—that is, to try to be constructive about it, and thus have the right death for me. To be clear about it and present during it. To embrace it.

The difficulty, however, was how to alter my perception of things, and then to make the necessary and frequent corrections as I altered it (in order to become more conscious) and to do that within the span of a short two or three months. To discover the secret, to revel in it and truly know it would require more than work. It would require unlearning and learning.

Fortunately, I'd already met two teachers. One I'd hired to help me when I was CEO. The other had been, for more than half a lifetime, my own personal Sherpa.

———

In my previous life, I had hired a consultant to help our firm with one of three agendas that, upon becoming chairman, I'd set out to accomplish—the most crucial of the three, the one that I hoped (when I thought about it) would be my legacy: helping our employees to live more balanced lives. And by the time I was diagnosed, we'd started to make real progress in that area, with very practical day-long seminars on how to achieve that; the seminars were held at various offices around the country, and partners and their spouses were invited. In my opinion, and that of many others, the most important note the consultant sounded was that we would have greater success in achieving our goals if we tried not so much to control time—an impossibility, as it is outside us—and instead tried to control energy—eminently possible, as it is within us.

Now, as I faced my greatest challenge, it seemed glaringly obvious that the same principle that had begun to improve our firm's culture—to improve the balance between work and personal life—could be of great use to me individually. I needed a new way of thinking about and looking at the world and at my own suddenly, shockingly abbreviated stay in it. A way that was not so time-dependent and future-directed sounded right.

And yet I had to come to this new mindset without, at the same time, abandoning my core beliefs. After all, up through that fifty-fourth spring of my life, my values and approach and overall philosophy, such as they were, had been incredibly effective, helping me to earn a prime spot in the workaday world. I felt a loyalty to who I'd been and what I stood for, even as I knew I had to open myself to something new. I could not merely discard whatever had gone into making up my basic self. Rather, I would need to redirect it, so that I might similarly "succeed" in the spiritual world, the world of my mind.

That redirection, I realized, would have to start with one of my most core values.

I had always been a great believer in commitment, in every aspect of life that mattered to me. Total commitment to marriage, to family, to country, to coworkers and firm, to neighbors and fellow human beings. To me, commitment equaled sacrifice, maturity, morality, certainty—virtues all, at least to me. Unfortunately, though, commitment, particularly in the business world, had come to equal time. Too often, your commitment was routinely measured by how many hours you were willing to work. By how much time you would take from your family. By how many years you were willing to live elsewhere, or manage one account. Commitment had come to mean reliability, proving that you'd been there already and promising to be there again. If you gave away huge amounts of your time, then it followed that you had exhibited commitment. If you did not give so much time, then by definition your level of commitment was suspect. Time alone was the bellwether.

Yet after our firm had worked with the consultant, and especially after my family and I had sleepwalked through the past couple of nightmarish weeks, I had come to wonder about the true nature of commitment. In fact, it's *not* about time. It's not about reliability and predictability. Commitment is about depth. It's about effort. It's about passion. It's about wanting to be in a certain place, and not somewhere else. Of course time is involved; it would be naïve and illogical to suggest otherwise. But commitment is best measured not by the *time* one is willing to *give up* but, more accurately, by the *energy* one wants to *put in*, by how present one is.

Once I came to this idea, I felt as if I were onto something. I could not control time. I had only partial control over my surroundings. What I could control was my energy. How I allocated it. How I used it in response to outside influences. This idea—this guiding principle—would help me to focus on what I needed to focus on. Consciousness, not commitment, was a better, more accurate, less time-entangled word to describe what I was always trying to move toward, from here to the end.

No more living in the future. (Or the past, for that matter—a problem for many people, although a lesser one for me.) I needed to stop living two months, a week, even a few hours ahead. Even a few minutes ahead. Sixty seconds from now is, in its way, as elusive as sixty years from now, and always will be. It is—was—exhausting to live in a world that never exists. Also kind of silly, since we happen to be blessed with such a fascinating one right here, right now.

I felt that if I could learn to stay in the present moment, to be fully conscious of my surroundings, I would buy myself lots of time that had *never* been available to me, not in all the years I was healthy. (Think of all those lost chunks of hours and weeks and years, all those lost moments. Now stop thinking about it. Don't dwell on it.) And while I could obviously do nothing to alter the bald fact that I had but three months to live (if that), by switching my mind-set I might well succeed in recalibrating, a switch that would help compensate me for what I'd lost in longevity with depth, quality, and intensity. The literal number of days available to me would not be great, but they would flow in a way they never had before.

Who makes such a fundamental change this late in the day?

I would soon discover, though, that staying in the present and being genuinely conscious of my surroundings were just about the hardest things I'd ever attempted. Making it to the top, running a firm of 20,000 people, even shooting par for the front nine—those were nothing compared to this. I wasn't alone in having trouble staying in the present. Two examples offered themselves, now that I'd become more sensitive to matters of time and our relation to it:

❖ A colleague of mine told me that each time he visited his elderly mother, who lived some hours away, the first thing she would say to him when he entered the house was, "When are you going to be back next?"

❖ My daughter Gina and I went to see *Batman Returns*. Both of us had a great two hours. The first thing she said when we got outside the movie theater? "I hope they make a sequel." She so desired (understandably) a continuation of the present moment that she wasn't really *in* the present moment! The hope for something that didn't yet exist had replaced the reality of the moment that did exist, a moment to be relished.

These may sound like loaded examples, but in fact I think they're perfectly universal. Who *doesn't* feel the desire, even compulsion, to know what's going to happen next? The need exists deeply in both the old and the young. Even a thirteen-year-old, who has so much more future to unroll out before her than her elders do, finds it difficult to live in the present.

Soon I started to identify whole breeds of people who did not live in the present, despite what they may have believed. They lived either in the future or in the past, or maybe nowhere at all. For example:

People who don't listen, who ask questions without waiting for the whole answers.

People who are angry and bitter.

People who, like me, thought they were looking at both the forest and the trees, but probably spent a little too much time on the trees. Or was it the forest?

Somehow, I had to learn how to be in the present moment, how to live there at least for snippets of time. Initially, I strayed. Constantly I strayed. Even when writing notes for this book, an endeavor almost completely driven by the knowledge of how few and precious were the hours left to me, my mind would invariably begin to stray to my previous work life, to business situations I'd faced but couldn't let go of. In my mind, the future and the past fought until they'd finally muscled out any chance of my experiencing something fresh and totally within my control—the present. Perhaps some of the continuing obsession with the future and the past, or even most of it, was motivated by ego, a basic and lifelong impulse to find one's slot, to still be seen as a contributing member of society. (How could I let go of that?) Or maybe the obsession was motivated by my being something of a micro-manager—after all, here I was, writing a book to tell people of my experience, and naturally that put me in mind of what I meant to tell a former colleague, or my nephew, or how to deal with that client . . .

Living in the present moment was tremendously difficult.

But it has to get easier, I told myself, *if you've been given a death sentence.*

Doesn't it?

———◇———

Every morning upon waking, I tried my hardest to be in the present moment. Just to appreciate what was around me, that very second. Because if I were in the present moment, I would not be so aware of time—time of day, time required to complete my remaining goals, time of year, time I had left. If I were in the present moment, I would be aware only of the experience I was having, not of how this might be the last time I would experience this, ever. If I were in the present moment, context and history wouldn't be the issues. The experience itself would.

I tried to be conscious of what was around me, really conscious, exclusively conscious.

I failed.

———◆———

My hot pursuit of the present seemed predicated on the idea that history and the past needed to recede into the background. Yet all I wanted to read (or, because of my deteriorating vision, listen to on tape) were books about history. In *How the Irish Saved Civilization*, I heard about how manuscripts from the crumbling Roman Empire were brought to monasteries on the then incredibly remote island of Ireland, where literate monks "saved" history from destruction.

Wasn't theirs simply a collective, cultural version of my individual ambition: the desire to attain as much consciousness as possible?

Could it be that the past and the present weren't as distinct from each other as I was making them? In fact, weren't they exactly the same thing . . . but for the little matter of time?

As I closed down my life, Corinne and I planned our final trip, for Gina and us. We would leave in mid-September, after the radiation treatments were done and I'd had a chance to get my energy back, as well as complete the other tasks I'd set out to do. I—we—chose three places with great significance to me: Prague, Rome and Venice. Prague because of its important historical and spiritual roots (during the Middle Ages, pilgrims passed through the city as they followed a trail to the holy lands); Rome because of its archaeological/historical roots (you could actually *see* how layers of history were built on top of each other); and Venice because it was both beautiful and dying. (It would also be a somewhat triumphant return to the opulent, sinking city, since Corinne and I had gone there as newlyweds with very little money, and would now be returning with credit cards.)

I had always loved reading history and appreciated the lessons it taught, if we listened. I'd always felt that, to live a meaningful, useful life, one had to feel that one was a part of history. Now, as I was dying, I realized that for all my authentic, even desperate pursuit of the present, I desired another feeling almost as much: the desire to be soaked in history, enveloped by it, where the very passage of centuries was visible.

The thought of the trip refreshed me. So much so, in fact, that I set for myself one more goal: to be well enough to attend the next KPMG partners' meeting, scheduled for early November—a couple of months past the time I was supposed to still be here.

I intended to be there.

———⊙———

I was convinced that I could learn something about the notion of controlling energy (rather than time) by recalling what we'd learned in those seminars the consultant had run. The concept was flourishing at the firm; why couldn't it work now, with me, in my current predicament?

We'd examined our culture to understand what mattered most to our partners. In interviews, our people articulated what they really valued. Their families, of course. To do work that was enjoyable. To have a life away from work. To be around smart, upbeat colleagues, in a team environment. To have an opportunity to mentor others.

Then we had interviewed spouses to hear what mattered to them. Only in this way, we believed, could we develop extraordinary professionals, because only in this way could we help them be extraordinary in other areas of life that mattered to them.

Then, to make ours a more compassionate, people-centered firm, we would need to create a new mindset throughout, an environment where, if you went on a well-earned vacation, you didn't feel like you had to check e-mail fourteen times a day. One where, if you left early on a Thursday afternoon to attend your daughter's soccer game, you didn't feel as if the entire firm would come apart. We looked at how we communicated internally.

How we multitasked. How we focused. We heard more than one story like this: A manager, his cell phone strapped to his hip, walks through the door after a three-day road trip, and the first thing he does—to his family's dismay—is check e-mail! Is that necessary? And yet, in his interview, when the manager was asked why he worked as hard as he did, he said, without hesitation, that it was because he loved his family! And he wanted them to know that! (Yet his clients had more access to him than his family did!)

Something was wrong. We knew we had to do a better job of connecting the firm's purpose with the individual's.

Through these seminars, we started advocating changes in behavior. The manager in this story, and those like him, would come to learn the simple, joyful ritual of having dinner with the cell phone turned off. They would come to see that—or the benefit of their families, themselves, and their firm—when they walked through the door, the first 30 minutes would be devoted, with *undivided* attention, to their family. (*After* that—the business world is incredibly competitive, after all—the manager could disengage for 15 or 20 minutes, check e-mail, maybe have a drink.)

In pursuit of greater balance, we started making improvements in physical and dietary habits. We learned about and advocated ways to get more sleep, enough sleep, the right kind of sleep. About walking or stretching or moving, in some fashion, at least every 90 minutes. (If you don't, we learned, the system starts to shut down, you tune out, and long business meetings become travesties, since few people can sustain the energy needed for them.) We learned that working out early in the morning is preferable, because oxygen transport is optimized. We learned not to go longer than four hours without food, in order to stabilize glucose and therefore avoid those sugar "crashes," after which one may technically be working but really isn't getting much done. We learned about eating often and lightly rather than infrequently and heavily. About drinking lots of water. In fact, we applied lots of principles from the sports world, whose practitioners, if they hope to be successful, had better know how to take care of themselves. (The consultant had worked with many world-class athletes.)

In short, the whole point of these modifications to our bodies and our habits was to help us feel more alive. To get the most out of each moment and day—for the firm's benefit and for the individual's—and not just pass through it.

Now I needed to do that for myself. I was confident I could because I had already seen it work, in gratifying ways, with our people. I'd seen partners succeed in creating a new way of being, by following the core of the whole philosophy: You can do anything if you give your best energy to it. Time truly becomes less important.

And yet—with good reason—there's nothing we're more obsessed with and addicted to than time. Time, whether it's well spent or not, whether it's enjoyed or not, just so long as it *is*. Many years ago, when Marianne was nine, she and I ran the famous San Francisco Bay-to-Breakers race together. (Every year several of us from the firm would do it; that year Marianne wanted to run, and I felt privileged to be her companion.) She did a tremendous job. During the race, we passed several kids from her school, and completed the course in a very respectable time.

The next day in school, she talked proudly about the accomplishment. "My dad and I ran the race in an hour and forty-five minutes," she said.

One of her classmates—a boy, probably not wanting to be upstaged by a girl—bragged, "Well, my dad and I ran it too, and it took us *two* hours, so we ran for longer than you."

———————

I wasn't able to focus. I still thought too much about work and the life I once lived. Yet each day, as work receded into the past, my focus began little by little to sharpen. The stress of my previous life faded a bit. I relaxed a little more. I enjoyed a little more.

A little, not a lot. I had a long way to go. (One of my closest friends, who had formerly been a top executive at multiple companies, said that when she retired, it took her a good *three years* to unwind from that life.)

I tried focusing again. I failed.

My continuing failure should not have surprised me. After all, I'd never been good at doing just one thing at a time. If I had a baseball game on, I was also having a conversation, and reading the paper, and periodically checking the stock ticker. My consciousness was frequently broken into small chunks.

Corinne, Gina, and I were privileged to be invited for a visit with Cardinal Egan, head of the New York Archdiocese. I figured that he had spent a great deal more time thinking about eternity and death and matters of the soul than I had, so I took advantage of the opportunity. In his private chambers, we celebrated communion, then we talked. I told him there had been much unfinished business when I had stepped down from my job. How could I learn to live—and die—with things still unresolved? I wanted desperately to live in the present—but how could I get past the past? "How can I stay in the moment?" I asked.

The cardinal told me that earlier in his career, he'd spent many years in Rome, becoming educated not just in the ways of Roman Catholicism, but also in the Italian mindset. And, much as he loved being Irish and so many things Irish, he'd come to appreciate a fundamental difference in perspective between what he saw as the Italian viewpoint and the Irish viewpoint. The typical Italian, he said, never went back over a decision he'd made; he felt as if that decision was the best one he could possibly have made given the information he possessed at the time, that while the choice he'd made might not have worked out as he'd hoped, it was the best decision at the time. "The only decision to focus on is the one you are still able to make," he said.

I nodded. We Irish suffer a long-standing tradition, if not a genetic predisposition, of looking back, of going over unresolved situations. "They say the only things the Irish take to their graves," I said, "are grudges."

Toward the end of our session together, I said to Cardinal Egan, "I feel a responsibility to die with as much consciousness as I possibly can." I did not phrase it as a question. I wanted to see his reaction.

"To those whom much is given, much is expected," he said. "Raise yourself to the highest degree of consciousness."

———

No disrespect meant to the cardinal, but later I couldn't help but think of the scene in *Caddyshack* where Bill Murray's character tells another character how he once caddied for the Dalai Lama, who stiffed him when the round was over. "Hey, Lama, how about a little something for the effort?" Murray asks.

To which the Dalai Lama says, "Oh, uh, there won't be any money, but when you die, on your deathbed, you will receive total consciousness."

Looking at the friend he's telling the story to, Bill Murray says, "So I got that goin' for me, which is nice."

Before my illness, I had considered commitment king among virtues. After I was diagnosed, I came to consider consciousness king among virtues. I began to feel that everyone's first responsibility was to be as conscious as possible all the time, especially later in life, especially toward the very end. For one thing, it could help others to understand the end better. That's a responsibility we owe to each other, certainly to the generation to follow. Maybe we'll discover that dying is something not quite so frightening. That would certainly be a nugget worth passing on. Maybe we'll discover that death is even something worth embracing.

Where once I had thought commitment could help change almost anything into a positive (and still thought that, to some extent), now I felt that consciousness could change anything into a positive.

———◇———

My wife was more practiced at dying than I was. Early in our marriage, she had worked in a Bay Area hospital and witnessed many people dying of AIDS, before AIDS was really even understood. She sat with them as they were dying. She saw how people who were very ill often gave up the will to live well before their body was going to fail. They were alive, but they were dead. It was a harrowing, eye-opening experience. Soon she began to delve into bigger questions about death and dying.

I felt extremely lucky to have Corinne with me—all the time, I mean, but particularly now. She would be by my side. She was my companion and friend and confidante, first and last.

But she would also be my Sherpa (I liked to call her), my spiritual guide to get me from this world to the next. Throughout our life together, her unwavering faith had instilled in me the courage I needed to get wherever I needed to go. Whatever balance I had enjoyed in my adult life I pretty much owed to her, to her contribution and wisdom. She would be the last person I would physically touch when I left this world.

To help me in my struggle to be in the present, she suggested that I "center" my consciousness—a skill that might help me to get there. Corinne had practiced meditation as well as studied cognitive science and psychology at Berkeley and Columbia. She had studied, and seemed to have an intuitive grasp of, how the mind functions on many levels.

"Close your eyes," she said. "Focus on the pineal gland, in the middle of your head, between your ears, behind the bridge of your nose."

Though it may seem out of character—even funny—for someone like me, I'd briefly practiced Transcendental

Meditation in the late 1970s when I was in Stanford Business School and Corinne and I first met. Once, she came by my apartment to find me in mid-meditation. Although she herself would come to understand the benefit of meditation and was far better at it than I, as she watched me hum on my couch that afternoon, she later told me, she seriously wondered if I was worth the effort.

Now, sitting on the rented couch in the unfamiliar living room of our new apartment (our new furniture wouldn't come for weeks), I did what my wife urged.

I closed my eyes. I'd probably be good at this exercise, I thought, since I often closed my eyes to stave off focal seizures in my visual cortex.

I imagined the spot exactly in the center of my head.

And I let go.

Or tried to.

My consciousness was not "centered" at all. Instead, in my mind's eye, my consciousness seemed to be lodged right behind my brow—a sign that I had not let go in the least.

"It's not working," I told Corinne, after a couple of wasted minutes.

Over the next few days, I tried it several more times. According to Corinne, some monks imagined a sideways figure eight—the infinity symbol—turning over and over in the middle of their head, to help them get centered.

Not me. Each time, I failed. I could get nowhere near the center of my head. Not even close.

If I was going to learn how to live in the present, if I was going to learn how to center my consciousness, I would have to get there via some other method. A trick, maybe. It would not be easy.

But that was okay. I was used to hard work. I relished it, always had. I was optimistic that I could do it. I was convinced that all of us had the innate ability to be conscious. (How could we not? Aren't we, first and last, conscious beings?) I knew that, as with so many other things I'd done in my life, practice would surely make me better at it. Consciousness is like a muscle, I thought, that would grow stronger when worked on.

But before I could succeed, maybe I first needed to discard my old ways. When I was a kid, if something upset me at school, I would come home, slam my books on the table, and rant for a bit, and my mother would just listen. After a while, I ceased ranting and went to do my homework and carry on with my day. She had a brilliance to her, an intuition, a mother's intuition; as I aired my grievances, she simply listened, saying almost nothing, because she understood innately that I needed to make the transition from one frame of mind before I could move on to another.

I had not yet moved on from my previous life.

I continued to struggle. I desperately wished for a way to be more present in the moment. I knew I had real consciousness in me. And I felt that my heart was in the right place.

That didn't mean I was going to get at it before the clock struck 12.

THE GOOD GOOD-BYE

"IT IS NEVER GOOD DWELLING ON GOOD-BYES,"
SHE SAID. "IT IS NOT THE BEING TOGETHER THAT
IT PROLONGS, IT IS THE PARTING."

—Elizabeth Asquith Bibesco,
"The Fir and the Palm"

My struggle to be in the present was not all-consum-
ing. (Maybe that's why it was a struggle.) There
were other things to accomplish while I was able. The most
important of these was saying good-bye.

About 13 years ago, around the time of my daughter
Gina's first birthday, my father was dying of lung cancer. I
flew from California to Florida to see him for what turned
out to be the last time. He was only 63, but he was pretty
accepting of what was happening to him. (Actually, it's

wrong of me to say it that way—as if there's an age after which someone would and should obviously be accepting of their impending death. I'm sure there are 88-year-olds and 103-year-olds who don't accept what is happening to them, and never would. As is their right.)

I don't remember my father conveying any formal wisdom in those last days we shared, about death or life or much else. We didn't talk about God. I wasn't asked to make any bedside promises, or to change my ways, or even to continue doing what I had always been doing. My dad was a pretty reserved guy. I do remember feeling that his acceptance, or seeming acceptance, of his death made it a little easier for me.

One of my tasks before I died was to "unwind," or close—or, as I saw it, *beautifully resolve*—my personal relationships. But why did I want to? Why would anyone want to make some kind of part-symbolic, part-literal break with all the people he had enjoyed and loved? I soon found out that not everyone with whom I attempted closure understood why I was doing it, or agreed with how I was doing it. But as soon as I started the process, it felt right. And it made me think that other people, especially those with much more than three months left (for example, several decades), could benefit from the approach I took, or at least modify it to make it their own.

The four reasons why I did it:

❖ I thought it would bring me and those with whom I was unwinding more pleasure than unhappiness (and, believe me, I realized just how much unhappiness would be involved).

❖ It would occupy me in an important way, making me think deeply about things I felt I should think about, things most people probably should think about.

❖ I was hard-wired by temperament and training for closure.

And last, and certainly not least,

❖ I could.

Let's start with the first reason: *It would bring me and those with whom I was unwinding more pleasure than unhappiness.*

This is really a two-parter. First, how could it bring *me* great pleasure? Simple. As I wrote down my list of people, those I intended to contact and plan a final encounter with, I stopped at each name and made myself recall, in the closest detail possible, all the moments the two of us had enjoyed together. How we met. What made us become friends in the first place. The qualities in them I particularly appreciated. The lessons I'd learned by knowing them. The ways in which having met him or her had made me a better person.

In short, the exercise forced me to do the very thing that wiser people every now and then advise us to do—that is, to stop and look up long enough to think about the people we love and why we love them, and to go and tell them *explicitly* how we feel, because who knows when that opportunity will disappear forever? (But that gets to my last point, and I don't want to get ahead of myself.)

The unwindings also made me feel good because they allowed me to remind myself of all the people whose lives *I* had touched, even if in a very small way. While quantity is not the end-all, I was surprised at how many people I came up with—and were you to try this exercise, you too might be surprised by your deceptively large circle. The sheer volume brought me tremendous fulfillment.

Part 2 of the first point: how could these unwindings really bring more pleasure than unhappiness to the other guy—or any pleasure at all? Wasn't I pushing miserable reality on him? Wasn't I asking her to do something that maybe she wanted no part of? (And not even asking, really, but practically commanding, since I was, after all, the guy who was dying.) Wouldn't quite a few of those on my closure list want very little to do with me—or, if not me, technically, then the mortality I represented?

As it turned out . . . no.

Sad and occasionally troubling as it was for some people (I'll talk about them in a bit) to correspond with me one last time, or to have one final meal with me, or to take a last walk in the park with me (which, it's worth noting, was sometimes not only the final time we would take such a leisurely walk together, but also the *first* time), I could soon enough see and hear how gratified they were to have this opportunity, this special time carved out just for us, exclusively to honor the unique bond that existed between us and no one else. Because of the gravity of the situation, my friends, colleagues, and acquaintances were forced to stop and remember what I'd meant to them and they to me. They were touched (sometimes overwhelmed) to know how much they had meant to me. I thanked them for having been in my life, for sharing with me their goodness and their talents. In these closings, I wanted to do something special for them, to make up for what I and we wouldn't get to do because I wouldn't be around. I wanted them to have something from me that would bring them a little pleasure, now and maybe later. For example, if I'd been a mentor to them, I wanted to do something to make them feel that they still had guidance. While I wanted us to focus, in these closings, as best we could on the pleasant memories, not the bad stuff, usually I didn't have to say a word; they knew it instinctively, as I think almost everyone knows it. It was never a hard thing for them to do. The optimist in me made me think that what was pleasant and constructive in our relationship wanted to triumph over what was sad and abrupt about its conclusion. For all the tears and choked-back words and the ominous shadow of finality that threatened to darken our encounters, the far more prevalent outpourings at these unwindings were smiles and laughter. If we were doing it face-to-face, I got to see it in their eyes. If it was on the phone, I could hear it in their voice. If it was by letter or e-mail, I could read it in their words. So long as the unwinding was done in a positive way, it often brought great comfort to both parties.

———◦———

My next reason why I wanted to unwind all my relationships, *because it made me think deeply about things I should think about,* is pretty obvious. Not only did these unwindings spur me to recall happy memories, but they kept my focus on life, not death. They kept my focus on my multiple connections to people, not my aloneness in the world. They kept me focused on connection, period, which— whether you are a person of faith, as I am, or not—is a balm. While I'd like to believe I wasn't someone given to triviality, my self-imposed mechanism for focusing on these important encounters, these unwindings, guaranteed that I was almost always thinking about what mattered.

Reason 3: *I did it because I believe in closure.*

Probably I don't need to explain this one; a guy who makes a to-do list two days after being told he has three months to live is clearly someone who likes and needs to tie things up. As a CEO, I had always felt that *nothing* could be truly effective—and often did not even exist—unless boundaries had been set, goals had been outlined, and a final result was evident. After all, my personal relationships were going to close with my death anyway, so why not do it in a way where I had more input? Yes, I realize that that sounds like a businessman talking, and that life tends to be messier than business. But maybe not as much as one would think. Could I have run my business well without having closure on all sorts of transactions—an account, a project, the fiscal year? Of course not. And with closure came satisfaction. *Proof* that something worthwhile had occurred. It was something, finally, that I could digest and understand, enjoy and appreciate and learn from. If the rules of baseball were changed so that a game didn't *have* to end after nine innings (with one team having more runs), the game would suddenly be far less interesting. Just because the baseball game that was my life was ending after six innings, not the regulation nine, did not allow me to pretend it wasn't ending.

Without closure, some (not all, but some) of my most important relationships might never be acknowledged and understood in the fullest way, either by me or by the other person. That would be a loss for both of us.

Now for my fourth and final reason: *I unwound my life because . . . I could.*

When I said, in the very first sentences of this book, that I was blessed by being told I had just months to live, I could not have been more serious. However tragic my situation may appear, I still got to do, as a final gesture, what most people can't: unwind all the relationships that meant something to me. Not everyone for whom death is imminent enjoys my other circumstances (still in prime, no physical pain, mostly mentally alert, loved ones nearby); in fact, I'd venture that relatively few such people do. Many of those who might be inclined to unwind their relationships in a way similar to what I'd planned probably wait too long and lose the chance. Most others may not even think about it and thus don't know what pleasure and insights they're missing (which I only discovered in the doing).

One of the great fortunes of my life, my prosperous American life—and I won't apologize for sounding sentimental or patriotic—was that I could experience real enjoyment in my final days, just as I had experienced enjoyment during my life. Simply because I was given the gift of being able to unwind my relationships, I did.

———

Okay, I realized there was one more reason, maybe the most important.

These closings allowed me to find balance in each relationship. That's not to say I kept a tally of gestures or kind acts, mine or anyone else's. But before I left this world, I needed to find equilibrium (if not find it, then create it) because I wasn't sure I'd lived a particularly balanced life, at least in the last several years. These closings would help me right myself.

One night, just a few days after the diagnosis had been confirmed, I sat down at the dining room table and on a legal pad drew this diagram.

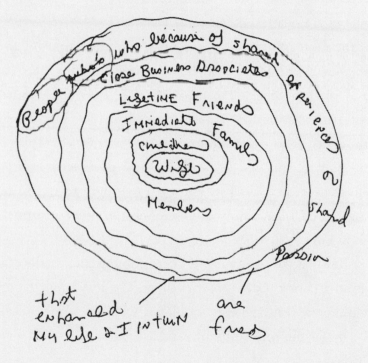

My plan was to start from the outside and work toward the center. After all, you can't unwind your most important relationships first, then bide your time with those loved ones while unwinding far less significant relationships, those with acquaintances and long-ago college room-mates; it makes no sense. Plus, the closer I got to dying, the more absolutely uninterrupted time I would want to spend with my immediate family. So I'd thought hard about the order.

Then again, a strong case could be made for doing it in reverse. Because if someone is fading (as I was, as most people with a death sentence are), then isn't it fair to wonder if the most important unwindings should go first and get the best energy? And only then, if there's anything left over, and you still feel so moved—only *then* unwind your less intimate relationships? And suppose I had less time than I thought (Who was I kidding? That was a very real possibility, goals left to accomplish or no goals left), and I'd spent precious days and energy unwinding relationships that were far less meaningful to me than those in my inner-most circles . . . what then?

But I had to choose. And I kept coming back to the diagram as I first drew it that evening. The good-byes to my children and my wife, it should go without saying, would be by far the most difficult, and it seemed right that they had to go last.

The next thing I resolved was to make these unwind-ings as special as I could. They couldn't merely be the last in a series of encounters. There had to be something about each that made it stand out, that compensated for the sad premise that lay just beneath the surface. I would make sure that the setting for our last encounter together was full of pleasure and pleasures. There would be good food and good wine. Or I would pick a beautiful spot for us to sit, by the water or in view of flowers. Or I would choose something appropriate to my companion, something that gave the unwinding the proper *theme*. For example, when I unwound with Scott, the son of a good friend and a terrific kid with whom we'd gone to a bunch of 49ers games when we lived in the Bay Area, he and I e-mailed each other with fond memories (including the time we'd scalped tickets). When that was done, in my final gesture to Scott, I went on eBay, bought a Joe Montana rookie card, and mailed it to him.

I didn't want to feel, or have the other person feel, as if I was doing this just so I could close the book on them. I wanted them to feel that this was a chapter they could not have expected, a rich and unforgettable one.

———

Unwinding the outermost of the five circles appeared to be a great gift.

This circle was made up of classmates, acquaintances, colleagues from years past, neighbors, good people from clubs and organizations I was part of, people who had enriched my life just by being in it and whose lives I believed I'd enhanced because of a shared experience or passion—business school, love of wine, charity work, the 49ers, etc. When I sat down to list all the people who merited inclusion in this circle, I was astounded to see that it came to almost one thousand. *1,000!* True, my leadership position, particularly in the last decade of my life, had put me in contact with many more people than the typical person. Even so, it proved to me that we touch the lives of many more people than we realize, especially since we tend not to be methodical bookkeepers (!) about it, but just keep a vague, occasional tally in our heads. It was amazing—even shocking, perhaps even tragic—that as we lived our lives, we could gradually forget so many of the people who had brought us small but wonderful experiences and joys throughout. And it was just as sad, too, that through our forgetfulness or carelessness or inability to stop for even a moment, we neglected ever to thank these people for what they did.

An unbelievable number, one thousand. I was able to conjure so many pleasant memories, memories that I hadn't thought of in years and that, had I not been diagnosed with inoperable brain cancer, I might never have thought of again, except for the occasional random association. I was amazed at how truly full and overlapping my life really had been.

It may seem a luxury to have spent more than just a little time on this circle, but it was very gratifying. I was glad for the opportunity to contact them.

> *Dear Martin,*
>
> *. . . I have cherished in particular the golf we played in the downpour in Scotland.*

> *Dear Steve,*
>
> *. . . The dinner we had at L'Impero was very special and complemented the conversation beautifully.*

> *Dear Richard and Elaine,*
>
> *. . . We've had the good fortune to share some great memories—especially skiing last year in Aspen.*

Still, I was dying. Because of that, and the incredibly large number of people in this outer ring, I couldn't "close" all of these relationships. Those that I did address— maybe half, maybe less than that—I closed (by necessity) almost exclusively through mail. A number of them I did by phone.

In each case, I expressed my appreciation and gratitude. And I tried to focus on something especially meaningful about our relationship. I attempted to turn the occasion into what I had come to think of as a Perfect Moment.

What was a Perfect Moment? Usually it was a surprise, though sometimes I could see it unfolding. Sometimes I could help to engineer it, by creating the circumstances that would allow it to happen, but the best details about it were still a mystery until they happened. A Perfect Moment was a little gift of a moment or an hour or an afternoon. Its actual length was never the issue. The key thing was that you had to be open to a Perfect Moment. The radiation machine breaks down; one hour is going to come and go, an hour you can hardly spare; but then you accept that machines break down. You don't get frustrated. You remember that it's a waste of energy. You focus instead on something pleasing. The rhythm of your own breathing. The intricacy of the face of the person seated across from you. The beautiful poem your daughter wrote called "Traveler's Fear." The color of the sky out the window.

Or you stroll with your wife past the Central Park Boathouse—already it's a Perfect Moment, a beautiful day. Such a beautiful day, in fact, that it's impossible to get a table at the boathouse restaurant, and normally you wouldn't even bother to ask. But that was before you were open to all kinds of moments. And so you ask. Somehow, a table has

opened. You sit down. The serendipity of the day's unfolding is making it perfect. But then halfway through the
meal, it starts to rain—a thunderstorm, torrential rain,
epic rain. Normally, you consider rain an inconvenience.
Something to plan around. But now you look at it as the
gift of rain, a treat of rain.

My openness to Perfect Moments, I realized, may have
been my own end-around at getting to consciousness, to
the present moment. And I hadn't seen it.

Which in itself was kind of perfect.

When unwinding my relationships, I tried to make
them Perfect Moments, too, or at least set things up so that
a Perfect Moment might happen. I called some people,
told them my news, and, not surprisingly, they were
shocked and saddened. But then I told them I was hopeful we could set up a time to speak about our friendship,
when I could let them know how much they had meant.
Most unwinding conversations turned out to be a tremendously two-way street—both for what we each brought
to it and for what we each got out of it. (I'm sure some
of you are thinking that it sounds incredibly one-way—
my way.) They were exciting conversations in that they
concerned things from the past, mostly good things, and
yet no conversations quite like them had ever before happened between us. I felt—and I think most people felt—
as if these unwindings offered the opportunity to create

something special, in the present, something that had not existed before. There was nothing stale about what we were doing. I may use the word *closing* about these experiences, but for the most part they were remarkably open. I may use the word *unwinding*, which implies a loosening, a falling away, and yet these conversations and experiences often bound me and the other person, especially those from the outermost circles, closer than we'd been in a long time. Maybe ever.

For example, take my college roommate, Doug, who'd become a journalist. We spoke maybe once a year now, but we shared a history, and we'd always enjoyed each other's company and were intrigued by what the other was doing. I wrote him a note.

Doug,

As you probably have heard, my health is failing me as I deal with advanced stage cancer. I wanted to write to tell you how much our friendship over the many years since Penn State has meant to me.

Best wishes in your life.

God bless,
Gene

I had planned to follow this with a call, to elaborate on my gratitude, but first I wanted to think about all the good memories we'd shared. The summer of our freshman year, when he and I had done ROTC duty on the U.S.S. *Wasp*, a WWII-era aircraft carrier, tracking Russian subs all over the Atlantic. How we played cards all the time against these two guys from Miami of Ohio. How we'd get served four meals a day and worked on the flight deck and in the boiler room, and how truly hot it could get there.

Doug called me first. No, he had not heard my news, and he was shocked by it, but we had a good conversation. We talked a little about the past. At one point, he reminded me that I had been the first among our group to reach a number of milestones—getting married, becoming a father—and now I was first to the next life. He and the other guys would be joining me later, he said.

Toward the end of the conversation, I told Doug how much I appreciated what he had added to my life. He did the same. I was not teary-eyed, nor, it sounded, was he.

"It is what it is," I said.

There were no fireworks involved in our conversation. No amazing chocolate cake or vistas overlooking the Grand Canyon. Yet it felt like a Perfect Moment nonetheless.

At the end, Doug said, "Good-bye." Not "Good luck" or "Keep the faith." No platitudes or denial. Just good-bye. I appreciated that.

———◆———

Given my attention to detail and my natural thorough-
ness, I had to remind myself how easy it could be to spend
lots of time with the outer circle, which would ultimately
be at the expense of the inner circles. I thought about how,
during my previous life, I might have unconsciously been
too consumed by the outermost circle. At work, with constant demands on my time, I'd got into the habit of meeting with certain people—good people, nice people, but
nonetheless fifth-circle people. Was it necessary to have
breakfast with them four times a month? I could have done
less of that. Had I somehow been inspired to draw my map
of concentric circles earlier in my life, when I thought I
had forever in front of me, I could have delineated for
myself how important certain people were and how less
important others were, and perhaps it would have guided
me in how I allocated my time (or my energy). Perhaps I
could have found time, in the last decade, to have had a
weekday lunch with my wife more than . . . twice? Where
had I found the nerve to press so hard for our firm to
rework its culture, encouraging our partners and employees to live more balanced lives, when my own was out
of balance?

I realized that being able to count a thousand people in
that fifth circle was not something to be proud of. It was
something to be wary of. Please don't misunderstand: the

fifth circle is nice. The people who populate it are worthwhile, and belong in the first circle of other people. They're just not the people who should have consumed the time and energy that they did.

I spent almost three weeks going through the fifth circle, then I was done with it.

By removing this layer, as with the next few layers, I was simplifying my life as I got down to the innermost circles. But three weeks was a lot of time to spend on the fifth circle for a man who had maybe three months. Too much time, actually.

I had miscalculated. I hoped it wouldn't come back to haunt me.

Time to move further inward.

———

Yes, the more I thought about it, the more I realized that while I was busy trying to be hyperconscious, to learn how to be in the present moment, I'd already started doing it. Just by letting go and enjoying what was right in front of me. Perhaps it seems dense of me not to have understood this right away. Then again, it made sense that I shouldn't have understood it at first.

In a Perfect Moment, time came close to standing still. A Perfect Moment could be an intense five-minute phone conversation. It could be a leisurely, four-hour meal with good wine and great conversation. It could conceivably go on and on and on because it wasn't the bounded moment you created; it was the proper atmosphere in which it could blossom.

The more I experienced Perfect Moments, the more I entertained the possibility of a Perfect Day, which was merely Perfect Moments strung together. In a perfect world, a Perfect Moment could last the duration of a waking day, maybe longer. Maybe the rest of one's life.

———※———

I marveled at how many Perfect Moments I was having now. I was getting better at it. It was beautiful. And as much as I had loved the hustle and bustle of my previous life, I couldn't help but think back on how rare such moments had been, and how plentiful they were now. Of course there had been Perfect Moments in my past. The day I married Corinne. The day I adopted Marianne. The day Gina was born. The day I became partner.

But almost all those moments one could have seen coming. They weren't the mundane, fabric-of-life stuff. Maybe other people appreciate the perfection in small moments (I'm sure many, many do) and I was just too caught up in my fast-paced, high-pressure life to ever get at the sublimeness that was embedded in them. I grant that that's possible. But it wasn't that the moments I was experiencing were about small things so much as that they caught me unaware. They were almost off-handed. In my previous life, the one where I couldn't have told you with certainty the year I would die, such spontaneous beauty happened rarely. Or I guess I was too busy to be open to it.

I did remember a Perfect Moment once in Scotland. I'd always loved playing golf there. A links course challenged you in a different way. Mounds that seemed to undulate like waves. Prevailing winds from the seaside. Rough like you've never seen. Daylight until past ten o'clock. The history and tradition. There was something magical about the courses. In fact, I thought it was more than just a feeling, but something almost tactile, as if the ground had an energy coming from it.

Once, when playing at Royal Dornoch, near Inverness, I felt a shock come up through the ground. I could actually feel the energy come right up my arm and through my hands. It was not an earthquake tremor. I felt extremely aware of something. I can't explain it any other way.

Subsequently, I found out I wasn't far off. Apparently, throughout Great Britain there are "lay lines"—veins in the Earth that give off electromagnetic or gravitational energy. These lay lines have been mapped, and their currents can be measured. (They're similar to underground routes of water that carry electromagnetic current; that's what divining rods detect.) Across Britain, many temples, including Stonehenge, were built atop some of the strongest lay lines. (The concept behind these lines is a cornerstone of the Chinese art of feng shui.) It's said that some people (not everyone) are sensitive to the current. I seemed to be. Corinne, too. Perhaps that was what made these courses magical. It certainly made that moment magical.

Now, I felt such heightened awareness frequently. Some people are especially sensitive to light, some to sound, some to smell, some to children or animals. I felt as if I was becoming sensitive simply to life itself.

———✦———

As my facility began to fade (slowly, I thought, very slowly), my occasional frustrations turned into what I thought was a business epiphany, about the great missed opportunity: Consumer products, I decided, needed to be made easier. Much, much easier. Too many things built into one device. Too many modes. I wanted simple. I had not expected to be infirm at this relatively early point in my life, when just months ago I was jetting between continents and putting in 90 hours a week and occasionally breaking 90 on the golf course . . . but here I was. And I was getting pretty damn annoyed at cell phones that did all kinds of things I didn't need, and whose operation was, for me, no longer quite intuitive. Camera mode versus noncamera mode confused me. I didn't buy a phone to have a camera. I bought a phone to have a phone. I didn't need down-loadable ring tones, games, Internet access. What I needed was an easy speed-dial calling list of all those people I might someday need in an emergency—my doctors, my family. I just wanted to use my phone to call people. Was that too much to ask? The young could multitask, but I couldn't, not anymore. I grew annoyed to think that American business had focused so incessantly on the youth market. Give me simple, simpler. And I was sure that the old and older and retired and unhealthy people in America wanted that, too. A simpler cell phone. A simpler computer. A simpler Blackberry. There was a market opportunity there, I felt. Go ahead, someone. Embrace "less is more" for those who need simplicity.

Was my deterioration starting to affect my judgment? Was I getting wise—or just cranky?

I didn't know. I just wanted an easy-to-use cell phone. One without a damn camera.

———

I remembered a moment from my past, a moment I hadn't seen coming. Also on the golf course. Walking down a fairway, alongside a small lake, at my favorite club, the Olympic outside San Francisco, a hawk swooped down just yards from me, plucked a fish from the water, and flew right by my head, disappearing past the treetops.

A Perfect Moment. I just didn't understand it at the time.

TRANSITION

———◦——

THERE IS NO DEATH! WHAT SEEMS SO IS TRANSITION;
THIS LIFE OF MORTAL BREATH
IS BUT A SUBURB OF THE LIFE ELYSIAN,
WHOSE PORTAL WE CALL DEATH.

—Henry Wadsworth Longfellow

Finally I had found what my thing was.
Water.

One morning, before radiation, Corinne and I went to the Cloisters, the medieval castle-museum on the Upper West Side of Manhattan. I had always liked it up there because of its lineage, its rich history. We sat in the high-walled courtyard adjacent to the herb garden. I decided to try centering my consciousness again.

This time it worked.

"Oh," I said. "The water. I can do it with the water."

There was a large stone fountain in the middle of the courtyard. Not only did the visual seduce me—its flow, its color or colorlessness, its braided movement—but so did its sound. Maybe even more so. Because of the high walls and the enclosed courtyard, the sound of the flowing water was especially transporting. Right away I knew I had found my spot.

Up to then I hadn't thought much about water. It held no special place in my life, as a kid or an adult. I was not a particularly good swimmer. I wasn't a sailor. My father-in-law, a serious sailor, once invited me out on his boat. I bought foul-weather gear (we would be sailing in San Francisco Bay), and when it came time, I enthusiastically hopped on board . . . and spent the entire trip bent over the side, retching or trying to. The first time I water-skied, I fell—and wouldn't or couldn't let go of the rope even though I was being dragged along the surface, bouncing, like a rag doll. So I was no water baby.

But apparently it was my medium. Looking at it and listening to it helped to quiet my mind, which aided my imagination of the present moment—or, more accurately, my quieter mind could move my thoughts to the next state, whatever that was. Maybe that's why it worked for me: because water, in its fluidity and frictionlessness, seemed by *nature* transitional.

Each day, I tried to spend a half-hour or more in an "altered state" of heightened consciousness, supported by the sight and sound of water, not really in the physical world, but not completely outside it, either. It felt in-between. Transitional.

First, I would look at the water. Then I would close my eyes. I would listen to the water. I would concentrate on the next world. I would experience what that world was like.

When I went to the Cloisters, I felt like I was returning someplace. It seemed as if it had been made for me. Sometimes you find what you're looking for in places you couldn't have guessed.

On days when I didn't have the energy to get to the Cloisters, I watched the East River from our living room, where, unfortunately, I wasn't aided by the sound of rushing water. On days when I was strong enough, we would be in my special spot in the Cloisters courtyard by ten in the morning. I would close my eyes and relax. Any muck that I still needed to let fall away would fall away. At first, I might stay in that "in-between" state for 30 minutes. Later, my meditation approached an hour. (Though I was not aware of how long I was in it: Corinne, who also meditated while I was in my state, would inform me afterward.)

Once I came out of it, she and I would sit there and I would describe the experience. I would tell her what insights I'd had about my life. Or if the state hadn't been as deep as I wanted, I'd talk about its quality. Once I asked her, "How do you know you're in the right place?"

"To me, it feels like my heart is going to burst," she said. "Like when you're incredibly excited, or in love."

"I don't feel that way," I said. That didn't mean it wasn't working for me, because it was. It was a state of complete peace. True tranquility. I liked being in that special place. I felt sharper when I came out of it.

Pleasant a state as it was, though, I never stayed in it longer than an hour. At a certain point, I would just know to withdraw from it, comfortable that I'd had enough. I wasn't ready to be kidnapped by angels. I wanted to get back to the world, do something with Corinne, see Gina, talk to Marianne, have fun. I wanted to eat a spectacular meal, more of the incredibly rich food and cholesterol-soaked desserts I'd been enjoying ever since I'd been diagnosed—thick juicy steaks, lots of ice cream, lots of cookies, lots of butter.

I wasn't dead yet.

———✦———

A river connects one place with another. That sounds simplistic, I know. But a river is nothing if not a connection. Yet that's not all it is. It can be more complex than that. It can change course.

I wish I could explain what I mean by that. But I can't.

———✦———

For weeks I'd been planning it.

The funeral would be held at St. James Episcopal Church, where Corinne and I had gone for prayer. My casket would be brought in by six pallbearers I'd already chosen. I hoped it meant as much to those wheeling in my casket that they'd been picked as it meant to me to have men of such character charged with the responsibility.

I selected the reverend I wanted to deliver the homily. I had liked the sermons he'd given.

I did *not* want organ music. Corinne suggested harp and flute. I liked the sound of that. Gina had played the flute since grade school.

In the crowd, there would be many family members and friends. KPMG colleagues and others from the business community. Tim Flynn, my good friend and successor, would deliver one of the eulogies. I hoped Stan O'Neal would give another one. I would ask him to speak not only because he was a dear and trusted friend, but because, as CEO of Merrill Lynch, he could talk a little bit about what work and responsibility had meant to me.

My kid brother William would deliver the last eulogy. He would say words from his heart, of course, but he would also include words I'd written over the previous months and sent to him, words to be delivered only after I was gone, words addressed to Corinne, Marianne, and Gina that I wanted said in front of everyone.

I really hoped that Gina would write a poem for the funeral. I didn't imagine she would be able to read it herself. Maybe her big sister would. Then again, maybe it would just be too hard to write such a poem.

I asked two close friends to organize the Irish wake to follow the funeral. It would be a celebration of life, a joyful gathering for all those people I loved. A chance for them to congregate and catch up with each other, share good memories, eat well, be conscious of the fact that they were together. All in all, to have a good feeling about life.

I hoped the weather would be nice, not more of the heat wave that New York had suffered through for much of the summer . . . then again, that was something I had no control over. But if I was lucky, there would be a clear blue sky with a little breeze, a perfect New York day. I wasn't sure, of course, if it would take place in the last days of summer, or if I might make it to the fall. I was fine with either.

I would be cremated. I wasn't yet sure what I wanted done with my ashes.

I knew there were plans afoot to have a separate memorial service in the Bay Area, soon after the funeral. I had many friends and business colleagues there, from my time at Stanford Business School and then my many years at the firm's San Francisco and Palo Alto offices. I didn't want my California friends to feel pressure to fly across the country for my funeral. During my unwinding with a KPMG part-

ner—a protégé and, most important, a friend much
respected by others at the firm—I asked her if she would
do me the favor of committing *only* to the California service, because her word would go a long way, and other Bay
Area people would not feel the burden (and expense) of
coming to New York to pay their last respects.

Planning it out this way, it was as close to being there as
I could get. I knew it would be perfect. Just like our wedding had been. Like Marianne's wedding had been.

I only wished I could be there.

———◆———

Sometimes I had trouble communicating verbally
and/or expressing my emotions. When these moments
came over me, it seemed (Corinne would tell me afterward)
as if my mind was in the shadows.

For me, the best analogy I could manage—the first one
that came to mind—was, again, a golf one, and it made me
think that "chasing daylight" was more than just a pretty
turn of phrase. When I went through one of these episodes,
I felt as if I was out on the course and I knew the ball was
there somewhere, but I couldn't find it.

———◆———

Why *can't* the last part of life be the best one? Yes, we
see elderly parents and grandparents dealing with the pain
and difficulties of aging. But if the physical pain can be
managed, who's to say this can't be the most spiritually and

intellectually rich time of our lives? Isn't it arrogant to pre-
sume it can't be?

Once, while playing in a tournament at the Monterey
Peninsula Club, I hit a shot off the tee, a par five. It looked
like a very good shot, but, unfortunately, the ball landed
next to a waste area. When I went to hit my second shot,
I missed the ball. Whiffed completely. Embarrassingly.
The whiff counted as a shot, of course. My third shot was
not much better, leaving me a good 200 yards from the
green. I hit my fourth shot and finally made it onto
the green.

As I walked onto the green, I couldn't find my ball . . .
had it rolled off? Had I sent it longer than I thought, into
the sand on the far side? I looked and looked and looked.

The ball was in the hole.

I'd made a birdie four on a par five, after one of my shots
was whiffed and another was almost as terrible.

A surprise, I think, is really just an inevitability that we're
too unsophisticated to predict.

———————

Closing my relationships with my most valued business
associates—friends—particularly those who worked at
KPMG, was especially satisfying. We'd shared a similar mission (improving our firm), and even though I wouldn't be
around to see it, my closings with each of them confirmed
what I'd already felt: that my professional mission would

be completed. That the bright future I'd worked so hard for would come about. I would be missed, I knew, but I was not irreplaceable. I was glad about that.

I told each of them how much I had enjoyed working with them and what they gave me.

I tried to do something special with each. One very talented young partner, someone I'd mentored over the years, I felt especially bad about leaving; she was going places, and I'd been both teacher and friend to her. During our unwinding, I told her my gift to her: I'd contacted a good friend, a well-respected executive roughly my age, and asked him to be available to her as I had (and would have) been, until such time as she no longer needed a mentor.

To be fair, I'm not sure who this gesture was meant for more. Her or me.

Another unwinding, with two close business friends. The heads, respectively, of KPMG's German and U.K. practices. Dinner, good wine, shared memories. We had a blast. At the end, we said good-bye, knowing we would never see each other again.

I went to the Museum of Modern Art with another close friend, someone who loved and collected art.

Stan O'Neal, his wife, Nancy, Corinne, and I shared a bottle of wine and talked about values. It was a beautiful unwinding.

One of my favorite places for unwinding was Central Park. Taking a stroll through the Ramble. Recounting the best memories and appreciating the best in each other.

One friend said he wanted to do our unwinding while we drove around in his new Maserati.

———⦿———

I felt simpler, quieter. More focused on the present.

But that didn't mean one should utterly ignore the future—especially someone with a lot more of one than I had. Almost all goals *require* a future. Without it, we can't plot a road toward fulfillment. I just felt as if the specter of the future often overwhelms us, to the exclusion of truly appreciating, and getting the most out of, the day, the hour, the moment we are inhabiting.

I hope my pursuit of awareness and of the present moment doesn't seem selfish to you, but it may. I did what I did as much for my loved ones as for myself. At least, that's what I intended. My daughter Marianne and my son-in-law William both worked extremely hard at their jobs and at home so they could give their children the best life possible; I appreciated the commitment and integrity they both displayed in building a solid future for their kids, my grandchildren. Then again, because of their devotion to building that future, they couldn't put much—time or money—into the present. Once, when Corinne and I took them out to dinner, Marianne wore a beautiful pastel-colored dress, one I hadn't seen before. She looked radiant.

"When was the last time you wore that?" I asked her.

"A year ago," she said.

"What sense does that make?" I asked. "You have a beautiful dress. You need to make more occasions to wear it."

But what seemed plain to me—that life had to be enjoyed as explicitly and as often as possible, *right now*—might, in reality, have been a little more complicated for those who didn't have just months to live. It takes hard work to build a future. It takes sacrifice. Yes, it's important to smell the roses whenever you can, but you can't do it every moment of the day. You just can't. In my new condition, I'd come to understand that when things were humming along, one's thinking could be self-absorbed and narrow. But I had to recognize that my new state could make me suffer the same tendency. I was looking at things through the lens of my condition. Wisdom doesn't always apply to every context.

I wasn't sure which part of me was the smart one anymore. Maybe, for the first time, I realized that consistency, a trait I had long esteemed, was sometimes not such a virtue after all. Spontaneity was coming up fast down the stretch.

When you get to this stage, of course you'll flail at first. After all, look what you're up against. But if you start to live in the present now, not only do you get to enjoy it (which is huge), but you also prepare yourself for the future, which someday will be your present, breathing in your face.

If you've practiced, you'll be able to live there. You'll have that muscle. It will be strong.

The present felt to me like a gift. (Perhaps I should say the present was a present.) Living in it now, maybe for the first time, I experienced more Perfect Moments and Perfect Days in two weeks than I had in the last five years, or than I probably would have in the next five years, had my life continued the way it was going before my diagnosis.

Look at your own calendar. Do you see Perfect Days ahead? Or could they be hidden and you have to find a way to unlock them? If I told you to aim to create 30 Perfect Days, could you? How long would it take? Thirty days? Six months? Ten years? Never?

I felt like I was living a week in a day, a month in a week, a year in a month.

Simplicity is in such scarce supply, I thought, yet so many people would benefit by it, be transformed by it. Looking at how some of the people around me had managed their lives, I lamented that they had not been blessed

as I had, with this jolt to life. They had no real motivation
or clear timeline to stop what they were so busy at, to step
back, to ask what exactly they were doing with their life.
Many of them had money; many of them had more money
than they needed. Why was it so scary to ask themselves
one simple question: *Why am I doing what I'm doing?* Part
of me understood the vortex, of course. Part of me understood that they couldn't stop, particularly if they'd enjoyed
success, because if they did stop, they would stop being
relevant. I understood. Completely.

But being relevant was not relevant.

At some point—a point it's preferable that *you* choose—
it's time to transition. To prepare for the final stage. I had
many friends that I worried would ignore that moment for
too long, try to stay relevant for too long, and then forever
lose the opportunity to control the choice. "Growing old
is a helpless hurt," Willie Mays said at the end of his career,
after a bitter final year in which he played like a shadow of
a shadow of himself.

It's coming, for sure. It's going to be hard, for sure. Some
people out there—not enough, but some—understand that
you start putting money away now, so that it can grow to
be sufficient for later in life, when you need it.

Why wouldn't you start doing that now with something
at least as important as your money—your soul?

<hr />

And where was the support for that kind of preparation? There are all kinds of medicines and medical devices and clinics and even hospice care to prolong life and make it as easeful as possible—but who helps you to really prepare for it, philosophically? Who teaches you how to embrace it? Is there anyone out there who really does that? And stays with you right to the end?

I was so fortunate to have Corinne by my side.

———

Unwinding relationships with close lifetime friends ran the gamut. It was easiest, I noticed, when my friends satisfied one or, more likely, both of these conditions: a belief in God or having an otherwise strong spiritual foundation, and a very solid marriage or partnership.

Those who didn't handle our closing well lacked both of the above. And often there was a third reason: they themselves were suffering through some big personal issue, and I served as a troubling reminder of how much they yet had to deal with. My leaving was going to create more of a hole in their lives, and they were angry about it. I understood that, and I had to ask myself, Whose desires should come first here? Mine or theirs? Was there a way to satisfy both of us, given that we each came pre-loaded with a very serious problem? I didn't know. But bringing our relationship to a close was difficult for both of us. Our conversation brought them not pleasure and a sense of richness, but

rather pain and anger. Of course I didn't mean that to happen, but neither could I help it. Nor did I think that for-
going our unwinding would be useful or even kind. It
wasn't going to make their pain disappear.

I had my rules. For each unwinding, I tried to create
boundaries. For example, I insisted we try our best to stay
in the present moment. (That didn't mean we couldn't
reminisce. Of course we could. Often it was almost all we
did. But it should be to relive the positives, the passion, not
an exercise in what-if.) And I was clear about the possibility for more of the same: there wouldn't be. (With my
innermost circles, there would and would not be, but I'll
explain that when I get there.)

Toward the end of some very good unwindings with
friends who were in a bad place, or in lousy marriages, or
didn't believe in some divine being or greater purpose, they
wanted to prolong our final encounter. They wanted me
to fight my disease more. They told me not to give up;
they thought I had. In a couple of cases, they continued to
call after the unwinding. They didn't want me to leave.

"I'd like this to be it," I would say. "I set this up specifically
so we could unwind. And we made a perfect moment out of
this. Let's take that and go forward. Let's not schedule another
one. Trying to improve on a perfect moment never works."

Not a popular answer. Too final. Kind of cold, actually.
The other person would often get emotional. Then again,

what happened if there was a standoff between us? The tie, I believe, goes to the dying man. Three years before, when my father-in-law was dying, he kept saying he was going to get better. I remember how I had wanted to say a conclusive good-bye to him, but he wouldn't look me in the eye. He was so connected to living that he was unable to accept the fact that at some point his life would end . . . and yet my need to bring our relationship to closure should not have trumped his desire to press on, however he chose to. He was the one dying.

Now, I was him. I was that man. I got to make the rules. As to rules for myself: when the encounter was over, I would think about it for a little while, maybe, sometime within the next few hours, then never again. (Later on, if someone asked me a question about the unwinding, or about that person, I would of course answer it, but I wouldn't return to it myself.)

I had to keep my eyes on what was in front of me. The road ahead was shortening by the day.

And those of my friends who remained troubled? They would just have to work through their problem after I left. Perhaps the unwinding was the thing they needed to give them the awareness and strength to do it.

Although I was not there yet, and perhaps was getting a little ahead of myself—something I had mostly stopped doing—my mind wandered often to my unwinding with

Gina. She and I were spending more time together than ever. She had recently turned 14, and, like anyone that age, she had her days. We'd frequently go out for delicious lunches, and we loved sharing our theories about religion and eternity and how we thought the mind works. But both of us could have short tempers, and obviously we were frustrated by what was happening. Sometimes it seemed insurmountable to her. Sometimes she seemed to accept it. I knew she was still forming as a person, but she was so aware of everything. I wanted her to understand my confidence and pride in, and profound love for her.

Whenever I thought specifically about our closing, I struggled to come up with the best way for a father to make his daughter see him for who he was, rather than for how long he had stayed.

I did not know what the next world would be like, of course. But the transition to it was watery, I felt, like a river. As I said earlier, I'd never before had a special feeling for water; it's not as if it was in me. Did my love of wine count? Wine was full of flavor (water is the stuff of life), wine took time to age and ripen (I was only now, at 53, truly understanding the universal pull of water), wine flowed through you (water flowed endlessly) . . . was there some analogy there?

But my growing feeling for water was really just that— a feeling, not an image. The Earth, and being in the earthly world, had a sensation unique to it. And so did water. Being in my altered, water-aided state for an hour or so each day felt different from being in the earthly world.

Marianne bought me a little water fountain, about two feet long and a foot high. I loved it.

So what lay downstream for me, or anyone? What would the next experience be like? Would everyone who's ever lived on Earth be there, in some form? Would I be meeting people from history I'd read about? Loved ones who had departed? I believed in a heaven, and also in a hell. I did not pretend to know where the boundary might be.

The next world felt beyond my comprehension, at least for now. But water? Water I understood. Water was my transition.

<hr>

No, that's not right. It's inaccurate to say water was my transition.

I was transitioning.

I was still living on Earth; I wanted to enjoy my time here; I was trying to live Perfect Moments and Perfect Days. But I also had to prepare myself. Every day, I had to spend some time getting ready for that. I had to put myself in my meditative space. I had to quiet myself. Simplify. Devote myself truly to preparing for the next adventure. But I still straddled, at best. It felt appropriate that when I worked at it, my eyes were halfway closed—still open to the light of this world, but partly shutting it out, too. I would go with Corinne to my walled courtyard and garden at the Cloisters, listening to the sound of my fountain. If I was too tired to go up there, and I had to do it from our living room, looking out at the East River, the experience started out as a visual rather than an auditory one, but it still fulfilled me. I would think about how the river, the water, was the connection between this reality and the next one.

Water is the flow between the two.

Water has no beginning or end. Water is continuity. Water is life.

I was far from having "mastered" the state. My goal was to stay in it, but sometimes I would get interrupted. My goal was to exist in this state completely, so that the future did not exist in my thoughts, but I wasn't always able to do that. Sometimes I would start to see my brain being under attack by the radiation. Or I would get pulled back by the experience of living. I was still like everybody else. I had more success when I tried to enter this state earlier in the day than later; when I started later, I would be more tired, and perhaps the numerous experiences of the day triggered thoughts of other things, things I couldn't control . . .

The better you get at it, and the more you do it, I thought, *the more comfort you will feel when the time comes.* I continued to work at it. That way, when my time came, it wouldn't be as bad. Maybe it wouldn't be bad, period. I was excited about my new exercise. I felt as if I was doing something spiritual *and* practical: easing the transition. If the next world was not completely separate from this one, but part of it—as I imagined—then by spending time transitioning each day, I was really shaping a path to it. My path.

Dying, I suddenly did not feel as helpless as I might have.

———

Spontaneity.

Perfect often seemed to go hand in hand with *unscheduled*. I had a Perfect Day with Corinne and Gina not just because I was with my wife and daughter, but because it had all unfolded without total planning. What would have happened had I let spontaneity play a greater part in my life? *Any* part in my life? Would I have sacrificed success in the business world, something that had given me so much pleasure and satisfaction?

Accounting is about predictability, about avoiding surprises. It's about, well, accountability. Wasn't there something "unaccountable" about spontaneity? Yet wasn't it part of life? To someone who'd lived as deliberately as I had, the idea was pretty sensational.

Skiing, I realized, was much more authentic than golf. In skiing, you just reacted. Skiing tolerated mistakes. It was more forgiving. You could make mistakes in skiing and still have a good run, maybe even a great one. In golf, you didn't have that luxury.

I loved golf. Don't misunderstand me. But maybe I should have done more skiing.

No one could say that, in my dying days, I wasn't still learning.

With my six weeks of radiation treatment finally completed, Corinne, Gina, and I went to Lake Tahoe, where we had a vacation home. At first, I was almost too weak to dress myself. After a few days of recovering from the radiation and the trip out west, I planned to start rebuilding my strength. There was a lap pool and weight machines. And I was looking forward to circling the golf course on a custom-made, three-wheel bike (my balance wasn't so good), at the impressive speed of five miles per hour. I was happy about the possibility of riding again, though I wasn't strong enough for a two-wheeler. I'd found my custom-made contraption on the Internet. It made me wonder if, as CEO, I had not availed myself enough of three-wheeled bikes—that is, creative solutions. I was pretty certain that the adventure I was going through now had made me a more creative, flexible thinker than I'd ever been.

I liked to think that I did a good job back when I was healthy. But had I known then what I knew now, maybe

I would have made a better executive. Almost certainly I would have been more creative in figuring out a way to live a more balanced life, to spend more time with my family. I always assumed you had to physically separate them. Home was home; the office the office. My thinking had been too narrow, my boundaries too strict.

While I wasn't one of those CEOs who felt he always had to be the hardest-working person at the firm, I certainly felt I had to be *one* of the hardest workers, or others in the firm would think less of my leadership.

But what if I hadn't worked so hard? What if, aside from doing my job and doing it well, I had actually used the bully pulpit of my position to be a role model for balance? Had I thought more about it at the time, I could have done it, could have been more creative. But I didn't. Not in the many years I was pushing. It took inoperable late-stage brain cancer to get me to examine things from this angle.

I heard about one CEO who lived close enough to his office that he inevitably found himself dropping by the office on weekends, and naturally ended up staying for hours, working. Why not, right?

But he got religion somehow. Something made him see that this was not the right way. So what did he do? He moved. Now he lived far enough from the office that he couldn't just drop in on weekends. While his new situation made for a longer daily commute, it also broke him of his weekend habit. He ended up spending that extra time with his wife and kids.

I had barely even considered limiting my office schedule. Yet had I done so intentionally, who's to say that, besides having more time with my family, I wouldn't also have been even *more* focused at work? *More* creative? *More* productive?

I wished I'd known then how to be and stay in the present, the way I now knew it.

Friends came to Tahoe who hadn't seen me since I was in the middle of radiation. We were all able to focus on the here and now—the staggering natural beauty around us, the amazing things. I wanted to enjoy each meal, each walk, each talk—not the future that loomed over everything, a future in which I played no physical part.

I wrote letters to my grandchildren—Oliver and Charlotte, ages five and three—in which I expressed my love for them, as well as my admiration for characteristics I saw in them that I'd always wished I had. I gave the letters to Corinne to give to the kids the day they graduated from high school.

More Perfect Days this week. I really thought that for most people (including me, before all this), it would take a decade to have as many Perfect Days as I had had in the past month. Since my diagnosis, not every day had been a Perfect Day, but the majority had been, maybe 75 percent. My goal was 100 percent.

I had decided that for the unwinding with Gina, we would do something special on the way to Prague (we planned to leave September 16). We would fly by private jet, which would require us to refuel somewhere in the far, far north, and that would give Gina an opportunity to meet and trade with the Inuits. That seemed to be a real hit with her. I expected my strength to hold out. Soon I would get word on whether the radiation had succeeded in shrinking the tumors.

I was gaining new appreciation for the processes of nature. Back when we lived in California, I had spent a lot more time outdoors—playing tennis, taking the occasional hike. Some of the golf courses I played on were rustic to the point of wilderness. But for the past several years, and certainly those years I'd been in the top spot, nature had become an afterthought.

Now, my appreciation for it had returned. I became much more sensitive to breeze. (Perhaps that was partly because I kept my eyes half or fully closed so much of the time, to quiet myself, to stave off focal seizures. The visual did not play quite the part it once did.) Having lunch at the club, just by the eighteenth green, I could hear voices, the sound of golf swings. I loved the rustling of the breeze through the pine needles. It sounded like water, the ocean. I smelled the pine. Birds in amazing blue and red circled about. Sitting in the same beautiful spot a year before, I would not have been as appreciative or even as aware of all the thrilling things that were so nearby.

For those who didn't get how the smaller pleasures can really mean more than the big ones, I now had six words: Drive for show, putt for dough.

But it would not be accurate to say that the transformation of my outlook since my illness was a newfound appreciation of smaller things. What could be bigger than nature? What could be bigger than water?

Good news: they called to say they thought the tumors had shrunk a bit. It was hard to tell for sure because of the swelling. When that subsided, they would know more.

I'm sure you want to know. What did it feel like to be in this spiritual world? Words are not sufficient, I'm sorry to say, but I will try.

It was incredibly enjoyable.

It was an environment with amazing energy, tranquility, love.

It was comforting.

There was no tension.

Whatever was required of me to reach this state did not feel (while I was in it) as if it required discipline. Rather, it felt like a natural progression.

After I was in this state, I could "remember" whatever natural phenomena existed in the area around me crisply—the touch of the breeze, the call of the birds, all of it. In a much more undiluted way.

When I was in this state, time retreated. Time stood still. I was no longer aware of having an experience; the experience itself had taken over. It was not me, it was the thing. The reward was in just being there, witness to it, but not entirely there. It was as if I had *become* consciousness. I was not in a transition, but—as I said before—I was transitioning *myself*.

I was reminded of a moment in college, in 1970, in the midst of the Vietnam War.

As an accounting major and straitlaced student at Penn State, I'd been appointed treasurer of the student body. I was responsible for disbursing funds to various student organizations. The left-wing Students for a Democratic Society (SDS) ran a slate of candidates for office, and their leader was elected student body president. In his new position, his stated objective was to mount various antiwar activities, and to do that, he sought funding from the student treasury. Though he'd been legitimately elected to office, it was against the rules to allocate funds provided by the government (Penn

State being a state school) for political purposes, such as
sponsoring radical speakers to come to campus. On the
other hand, he was the elected leader, and spending money
on items like printing or microphones was within his rights.
I told him he could have the money for that, but he would
have to raise other funds if he wanted to spend it, say, on
bringing radical speakers to campus. One Saturday night, he
raised ten thousand dollars by screening the counterculture
classic *Reefer Madness* to a sold-out crowd of stoned students.
I carried shopping bags of cash, from the night's take, back
to my fraternity house; Monday morning I deposited the
money in the bank and then gave him his funds.

What in the world could this memory possibly have to do
with the Other Side? With the transition? *My* transition?

It struck me that this story exemplified how you can
hold on to who you are while also modifying your thinking. It was about staying rooted while also growing. It was
about having one foot planted on firm, familiar ground,
while another toed new and unfamiliar ground. It was
about how, if I was going to transition to a different world,
I needed to transition myself.

Norman Vincent Peale once said, "Change your
thoughts and you change your world." As a hard-charging
businessman, a former CEO, I was powerless to change the
turn my life had taken. Fortunately, I had the power to
make things better. I still had power over me.

⎯⎯⎯◈⎯⎯⎯

The shadows had not yet overtaken me. There was still light. I continued to have good cognition, felt as if I could entertain "big-picture" issues. But my speech, my appearance, and my ability to do little, everyday tasks were increasingly affected. Dealing with the functions on my cordless phone was a trial. The same with getting dressed in the morning. Yet it was precisely *because* of these frustrations—not despite them—that I understood again one of the key ways into a Perfect Moment: acceptance. The end result—the goal—of a Perfect Moment was to taste as much of the flavor that life is constantly offering. But the *way* to all that was through acceptance.

When I was having a particularly good day, a day made up of many Perfect Moments, I would always remember that it was precisely *because* I didn't manage everybody and everything. Coming from a recently departed CEO, that was quite an epiphany! My strength was diminishing. I could not even load a CD into the player to hear my books. But by letting go of the quirks and delays and inconveniences of every day, I started to learn how to enter—and eventually to linger in—the present moment.

⎯⎯⎯◈⎯⎯⎯

The tumor had shrunk. It looked like I could travel to Prague.

⎯⎯⎯◈⎯⎯⎯

It was the best day of my life.

We took a boat out on Lake Tahoe. For the first time when riding in a boat, I sat in front, the only place Gina ever sits. There, I found it a much more visual experience. The water looked like glass. There were hardly any other boats out, or it seemed that way. Maybe we moved at 30 miles an hour, I don't know. We crossed the lake. We seemed to be riding not in the water but on it, skating along the surface. It seemed as if I was part of the water. It went on for miles and miles.

I loved the sensation of being so close to the water. Or really, it wasn't so much that I *loved* anything, but just that I *had* the sensation, felt it fully.

Corinne and I decided that afternoon that we would both have our ashes spread upon the waters of Emerald Bay, in a very particular spot that we loved.

Corinne, Gina, and I took a friend on a drive around the golf course because it was late in the day and we wanted him to enjoy that moment of serenity and flat light and giant shadows, and we wanted to enjoy it, too. Gina was happy to be behind the wheel of the cart. What 14-year-old wouldn't be?

There were only a couple of foursomes on the course. As one golfer prepared to hit, Gina stopped the cart and we all watched. Corinne, a fine golfer, couldn't help but be aware of whether his swing was good or bad, but I didn't notice that part of it at all. Which wasn't surprising. As much as Corinne had been more than just my partner but my soulmate—just about literally, joining me in prayer and meditation and every part of this journey—during those last months, she was obviously in a different place. As was almost everyone I knew.

As we drove around, the shadows gradually grew longer, a subtle but definite change. The trees seemed to grow bigger and more peaceful. In the past, whenever we would play during that time of day (either Corinne and me, or me and a friend) and I struck the ball, I felt as if I were hitting into a picture, into something two-dimensional. The ball would be harder to locate, I knew, even if I had put it in the middle of the fairway. Because there was so much more stillness at that peaceful time of day—so unlike a morning round, with lawnmowers buzzing and sprinklers spinning and lots of other energetic golfers striding along—golf felt like more of a personal challenge than usual, as if its essence had been boiled down even further, to some super-essence: just you (and maybe a partner) and the course, the ball becoming harder and harder to hold onto—sometimes its flight becoming impossible to follow, sometimes the ball half in sunlight, half in shadows. And as you moved toward the latter holes on the back nine, you realized, slowly, yet with a certain amount of excitement and even joy, that it was just you on the course. No one else was left. It was no longer late afternoon but the gloaming. Your fellow players had been replaced by fellow shadows.

We returned the cart to the pro shop. It was time for dinner. The young club pro in the shop came over to shake my hand and agreed to go with me to the back of the driving range in a week or two, whenever I felt strong enough, so we could see if I could still swing a club and hit a ball.

———◦———

Everyone loses his or her game periodically. When it happened to me, I loved how my fellow golfers, no matter how naturally competitive, would support me, trying to help me get my game back. Or, if it looked as if I wanted to be left alone to get through the struggle myself, they would leave me alone.

———◦———

I was zeroing in on my perfect time of day. I was getting closer to zero miles an hour. Yet as slowly as I was moving, I was chasing. The last rays of light and the shadows that fall just before the gloaming that follows. Gloaming is when shadows disappear. It's not completely dark yet, but there are no more shadows. Gloaming is what separates day from night. Just you and the course, playing by yourself, harder to follow the flight, light is flatter, more like a painting, drawing of the shadows, your ball half in shadow, half in sunlight. Sun is low. Shadows get longer and longer, greater challenge. Trees grow bigger. More peaceful. No one on the course. Just yourself. Just before the gloaming. More and more shadows.

———◈———

I was having more frequent "episodes." There was no mistaking that they were harbingers. I was feeling much weaker. When I walked, I had to put my arm around Corinne's shoulder and lean on her. I spent more time in bed.

———◈———

We rented a boat and went out for another day on the lake—Corinne, Gina, my sister-in-law Darlene, my nephew Corwin. We talked about many things, including God. Corwin, 25 and an engineer, a brilliant young man who rejects the church and doesn't believe in God, said that he believed in science. For him to believe in the existence of something, he said, it had to be testable, provable. His lack of faith in God troubled me for two reasons: he's so smart, and he's young. Since I had become sick, I'd become dramatically less interested in the opinions of people my age and older, and more interested in the opinions of those younger—Corwin, Gina, Marianne, and other young people whose very youthfulness, it seemed to me, made them worth listening to. What did they think of the world and its future? Their more pliable minds made what they had to say more relevant than what my peers or I did.

It was a lively discussion. When we got off the boat, I turned to Corinne. "This has been the best day of my life," I said. I meant it.

That night after dinner, I became extremely agitated. Darlene and Corwin had a four-hour drive back to the Bay Area, but I wouldn't let them leave until I cleared something up. I sat everyone down.

"Okay, I understand that one doesn't have to believe in God," I said. "But I want to understand how you *can't* believe in God. Isn't that the same as consciously making the decision not to let love into your life?"

Corwin said he thought my theory was off in that I seemed to put love second to God. He said that a person did not need to believe in God in order to love and be a person of faith.

The conversation did not end satisfactorily for me. I was frustrated by the impasse. Later, when Corinne and I were alone, she said, "Some of us think that God *is* love."

I felt a little clearer after that.

———

I saw the hawk swooping down beside me on the fairway, so close I felt like I could grab it. The hawk plucked the fish from the lake just yards from me, so close I felt like I could have plucked the fish. The hawk, fish in mouth, rose into the sky and disappeared beyond treetops.

The unwinding with Gina needed to be more special than anything else I'd done. She was a poet, an inventor, a brilliant mind. She was my daughter. I needed it to be as poetic as she was, and as spectacular.

The day had turned.

—————◦◊◦—————

My mother and my brother flew to Tahoe for our final "unwinding" weekend. I'd already said the physical good-bye with my sisters, Rose and Linda. They could still phone me if they wanted to, and they did, and we would talk. To "close" with those in my innermost circle meant, as it did with others, that I had expressed what I needed to and that I had made my peace with them. It did *not* mean that we couldn't speak after that; it meant that I had tucked something away for good, something untouchable, something perfect.

On Saturday, we had good meals together and nice conversations, but I needed to rest.

On Sunday, we rented a boat and took Mom and William out on the beautiful lake. I'd thought hard about what to do with them for the weekend, and I chose the boat ride because I thought that would be best and most exciting and relaxing for them, and of course Corinne and I would have a great time. If it was special for them, then there was a better chance to make a lasting and happy memory for them—something tangible and enduring that enabled me to feel as if I was reaching out to them beyond our mere physical parting. The week before, Corinne, Gina, and I had been out on the lake with Darlene and Corwin, and I remembered it as the best day of my life, one among many these days. All stress seemed to evaporate. I didn't see any reason why this day on the boat with Mom and William couldn't match that day.

After we were out there a while, I took my mother's hand and walked her to the front of the boat to talk, just the two of us. I told her I was in a good place. I told her I would see her in heaven. A person of deep faith, she was comfortable with that.

Later, my brother and I talked alone. He was angry— not at me but at life, that this should be happening to me.

"Your anger won't do anyone any good," I told him. It would dissipate him, I said. He needed to try and live in the present. I told him to take the energy he was spending being angry at the world, double it, and channel it into love for his children (or even *more* love, I should say, because William already loved his daughters and son dearly).

He promised me he would. I told my brother how proud I was of him. I told him what a great father I thought he was, and how great a dad he would continue to be.

It was a perfect day. I felt complete. Spent but complete.

CHASING DAYLIGHT

---◦◦◦---

By Corinne O'Kelly

By late summer, the unwindings were taking their toll
on Gene. While I had watched him decline steadily,
the pace picked up by the end of our time at Lake Tahoe.
Gene was still capable of remarkable lucidity, thanks in large
part to his inner strength and courage, but understanding
what he was trying to get across was getting harder. He was
less frequently conveying thoughts in the generally logical,
ordered way he had done up to this point. Some discussion
was often required before his meaning became clear to me.
To preserve the authenticity of Gene's experience, I metic-
ulously took notes of our exchanges.

One of our last nights in Tahoe, I felt Gene starting to go. He just suddenly felt far away. It was the evening after his mother and brother had left. I was lying on the couch, in his arms. I commented on his "absence," and he responded, "You're going to have to take over now. I've done all I can do."

It took my breath away.

The next night in the den, Gene, Gina, Caryn (Gene's assistant), and I watched a movie. He was reclining in a big leather chair, and I sat in front of him, in a beanbag chair on the floor. I held his foot the whole time. Every few minutes I turned to look up at him.

Then Gene began to shake violently.

I called for Caryn to get Gina out of the room. With all that our daughter had seen her father go through over the past months, I didn't want to add to it the haunting image of him trembling and shuddering and quaking through a grand mal seizure. He was trying to call my name; I felt helpless. Thankfully, Caryn had witnessed such a seizure before, which gave me some comfort.

I called 911. The seizure was over in five minutes. The ambulance came. We spent three hours in the emergency room in the hospital in Reno.

The next day at the hospital, Gene recalled that he had felt no pain during the seizure. Nor had he felt frightened. But he was determined to avoid another one.

"So how do people travel if they might have seizures?" he asked.

I surmised that they'd probably need a medically equipped plane, with a doctor on board. In Gene-like fashion, it took him about three seconds to figure out that he'd finally bumped up against a limitation that couldn't be beat. That he would not accomplish his next goal—taking Gina to Prague.

And it was that that signaled the beginning of his transition. He had come to realize that all the things he'd planned still to do, he couldn't. He began to accept the limitations of his failing body. He realized it would be too difficult and draining to travel to Europe.

He looked at me. "Promise you'll take Gina to Prague," he said.

I promised him.

———⊙———

At the hospital, Marianne and her father started their closing. A grown woman and a parent herself, Marianne understood that life and marriage and parenthood were not so simple, and she appreciated her father's sacrifices in a new way. She also had a fresh appreciation for one of his most distinctive qualities—a "cut to the chase" approach that had made him so successful in business but could sometimes come off as abrupt in personal interactions. In the last few years, when Gene was constantly on the go and Marianne was in California raising two small children, he would call her once a week, usually while being driven to the airport for a business trip. Rather than making small talk, he'd right away want to hear about her internal struggles, what really was bothering her or making her happy.

Now, at the Reno hospital, she and her father, for the first time in decades, had uninterrupted time to talk (in between Gene's catnaps). It was wonderful, frivolous conversation, something they'd rarely indulged in. They spent a half hour just comparing notes on how much they each loved to eat gooey cheese, actually talked and laughed about it for a half hour. It wasn't important in the slightest, which made it all the better. They talked about everything. Gene wanted to talk about when Marianne was a little girl. He said things he'd never voiced before. He talked about what a good mother he'd been blessed with, how patient and caring and energetic she was. He got especially emotional talking about his father. He was sad about their relationship. While he knew how seriously his father had taken the responsibility to provide for his family, it hurt Gene that his father hadn't been more affectionate.

For Marianne, there was a satisfying consistency to see her father dying in this manner: focusing hard only on what mattered.

After two nights in the Reno hospital, we flew to New York, where Gene was admitted to Sloan-Kettering Hospital. The doctors thought he could go home after a night or two, but because it was the Labor Day weekend, we knew he would probably not be discharged until at least Tuesday.

The weekend was a nightmare. Gene was deteriorating as his appetite and strength diminished. Because of the long weekend, the hospital staff was severely reduced. I stayed at the hospital around the clock.

The Tuesday the doctors returned from the long weekend, tests revealed that Gene's seizure had been precipitated by a pulmonary embolism. He was given a blood thinner to reduce the chance of another. He also developed pneumonia and became noticeably weaker. His body was seriously starting to fail. He was aware of it.

The doctors wanted to take a sonogram of his stomach.

"No more tests," he told them. He was not getting out of bed for that.

It made sense. Staying alive at all costs was not the goal—not anymore—and he didn't want to waste any energy enduring medical procedures that, at this stage, were pointless.

This marked the next stage of Gene's transition. He was truly shifting from the plans of the living to an acceptance that he was dying. To die in peace, you first must accept that you're dying.

———◦———

Gene rarely spoke except to me or the doctors.

"I've had a great life," he said to me as we lay in each other's arms in the cramped hospital bed.

We talked of other very personal things. We talked about the book—how it would be the culmination of 30 years of teamwork. He told me how my insights on death and dying had helped him transcend his fear. As a health-care provider who had witnessed death routinely, I had come to realize that if you conquer your fear, you conquer your death. I had assisted dying patients in understanding that when you are motivated by fear, you are not able to see the best path—whether in death or in life. This had been my clearest message to Gene during the past three months.

He was embracing it, finally.

———◦———

It was that day, Tuesday, September 6, that he stopped wanting food. It was also the day he said to me, "I think tonight's the night I will die."

"That would be something for the book," I said wryly. "You were trying to maximize and manage all you could about your death. Predicting the actual time you died would make quite an ending."

He smiled. So did I.

"I don't know that you can control so much," I said. "The body is amazing, and the mind is even more amazing. But I'm not sure you can make your body do exactly what you want. Even for a good ending."

The head of Psychiatry dropped in for a visit. The three of us talked for a few minutes. I shared with him Gene's pronouncement that he was going to die that very night and asked the doctor if this was something he had witnessed before. He said that some people have a sense of their impending death.

But Gene didn't die that day. Although he was ready, he would have to wait until his body failed. As sick and weak as he was, he was still a young man with a strong heart.

All the hospice personnel expressed their amazement at Gene's tranquility and the way in which our family was creating the best possible scenario for his death.

On Wednesday, Gene didn't die, either. It was the day we were finally able to bring him home, where he so desperately wanted to be.

Back at our New York apartment, the one we'd rented just three months before and hadn't even moved into when Gene was diagnosed, a hospital bed was brought in. He would die at home, where most people would die if they could. He expressed his awareness of how unfair it was and how lucky he was—that other people didn't have the

means to be taken care of at home, to have a nurse looking after them in their final days. How their hospital bed
was in a hospital. Probably they had to share a room with
a stranger or strangers, with the families of those strangers
coming and going day and night. Probably their care, while
maybe excellent and compassionate, was intermittent, at
best. Gene was aware of all that.

He stopped asking for water. It wasn't forced on him
because he had said more than once that he didn't want to
be medicated at the end.

He had been opening his eyes less and less over the previous weeks; now he hardly opened them at all. Only at
special moments.

On Thursday, a doctor from Visiting Nurse Service of
New York—a hospice service—came to our house. He
spent a little time with Gene. Later, he told me that, in the
six years he'd been doing full-time hospice work, he had
seen numerous people, younger and older, with primary
brain tumors like Gene's, and that they often experience
"terminal restlessness" or "end-stage restlessness," an agitated state that frequently requires heavy medication—
antipsychotics, opioids, and benzodiazepines (tranquiliz-
ers). This state is caused by a combination of factors. It
might be fluid pressure on nerve impulses or something
else physical. Or its source may be social or spiritual.
When young people experience this restlessness, it's often

because of the things they neglected to do—not just regrets about unfulfilled dreams and dashed expectations and things untried, but also the good-byes, the closures. A lot of people arrive at that final stage having not done the psychosocial and spiritual work that would have brought them more peace. It's true for older people, but especially for "young people" like Gene. The doctor realized that Gene's "unwinding" plan was somewhat compulsive and seriously Type A—wanting to tie *everything* up, as if that were possible—but that ultimately it was positive. The doctor couldn't help but compare Gene's attitude with that of another man he had recently tended, a very senior executive at one of the big pharmaceutical companies. This man was about 60, not particularly close with his family, not close to his children, with no real spiritual foundation—and he would talk and mumble and even cry out in the middle of the night, angrily barking the names of colleagues and superiors (his CEO was the preferred whipping boy). His rantings were deeply upsetting to his wife and to others who came to see him at the end. The man had to be heavily medicated. He died restless.

Gene was fortunate not to have physical pain, but he had also done himself and those around him a hugely positive thing by resolving his relationships and embracing what was happening to him.

"Your husband isn't agitated," the hospice doctor said. "He's peaceful."

———◦———

One visitor that afternoon asked Gene if he felt peaceful.

"Yes," he said.

The visitor asked him if he felt pain.

"No," he said. Gene said he felt no pain in his brain, no pain from lack of food and water. Nor was he feeling fear.

"Is this the transition?" the visitor asked.

"Yes," said Gene.

"Are you in a good place?"

"I'm in a great place," he said. All his life, Gene had only ever said things he meant, and that was not changing now. If anything, he felt things more deeply than ever before.

After a long moment of silence, Gene said, "I feel supported on the other side."

I did not ask him what he meant by this. It seemed to me that he had made some positive connection to the "other side." And that his soul was involved in the transition.

He rested. The visitor and I left to talk in the living room.

About a half-hour later, Gene, his eyes wide—wider than he'd opened them for days, according to my sister, who saw them—called to Darlene. He looked at her, alert as ever.

"Please tell them," said Gene, "that there is no pain between this side and the other side."

———◦———

Later, Gene asked Marianne to run to Starbucks and get him an iced coffee. She came back and he sipped some. Then he asked for orange juice from Starbucks. Marianne ran right out. These were the first liquids Gene had asked for in days. The doctor explained to me that because Gene had not been taking in much fluid, he was becoming dehydrated, so the swelling in his brain was going down; because of this, Gene—just like anyone going through this situation—appeared to be improving. After a relatively brief and charmed period of this, the doctor said, there would be a final decline.

At some point that day, Gina, Marianne, and I were seated around Gene's bed. He looked at the three of us.

"That's the most beautiful sight in the world," he said.

———◦———

Later, I was working at the computer in the other room when the nurse came in. Gene wanted me, she said. When I reached his bedside he said, "I can't find the river."

"Do you want to look out the window?" I asked. "To see the river?"

"No," he said. "I can't *find* the river."

Near his bed I set up his water fountain, the one Marianne had bought for him. A few minutes later, with the fountain going, he said, "That's much better."

A moment or so after that, he said, "I can't find the river." And a moment after that, again with agitation in his voice, he said, "I can't find the river."

I held his hand. I sat with him a long time.

"I can connect with you and I can connect with God's love," he said, after a while, "but I have trouble staying connected to the river. You can easily connect to the river. Stay connected to the river and I will stay connected to you and God and I can find my way."

He slept. The rest of the night passed peacefully.

———◦———

He struggled the next morning, Friday, as he'd struggled the day before, to find and stay connected to the water and what the water represented. The struggle was about something.

It had been my experience that a dying person often has one or two things that weigh particularly heavily on him or her at the end. Once, I'd worked with a man who had been suffering for two years from the effects of AIDS. In his final hours, he held on so that he could see his mother one last time; he knew she was on a plane rushing to his side. Two hours after she arrived, he died. Of course, many people die without those issues being resolved. Eventually the body wears out.

From the moment of Gene's diagnosis, he had expressed deep concern about how I would get through the first six months after his passing. He was concerned that I would suffer a broken heart.

I knew that that continued to weigh on him.

Gene's sisters, Rose and Linda, arrived. He was able to have special moments with both of them.

In the afternoon, he wanted me to make sure that his legs were raised 20 degrees and his head 40 degrees.

"Why?" I asked.

"The body you come in with is connected to the water," he said. "When it leaves, he wants to be in this position . . . it would be best for leaving the body."

This idea is reminiscent of an idea put forth by Tibetan monks, who believe that when you die, you should be sitting up because consciousness exits the body at the highest point, and if it leaves from your head, you will be most conscious, which will enable you to have greater influence over your reincarnation. It was impossible to say with certainty whether he had ever read or heard about this Tibetan concept, or if it came to him from another source, or if it came to him from no source but his own.

"Where did you get this idea?" I asked him.

"It just seems right," he said.

———◆———

Now and then Gene would take a sip of his coffee or orange juice. The reverend came to visit him. Gene's sisters spent time with him. Marianne and Gina spent time with him.

As demanding as the experience was on Gene, he still worried about my well-being. When I asked him if he would like me to hold his hand through the night, he said, "If it would not tire you too much."

We lay in separate beds, his hospital bed placed next to what had been ours, and I held his hand through the night.

———◆———

On Saturday, my brother Donald drove down from Massachusetts. He and Gene talked in the bedroom. When Donald came out, he said that Gene was worried about me, about how his leaving would affect me. Donald said he had assured Gene that I would be okay, and that he would watch out for me.

Marianne left. As soon as she got on the plane, she would tell me later on the phone, she wished she had stayed.

Others stopped by during the day. It clearly took great effort for Gene to respond.

When Caryn, Gene's assistant of eight years, visited for the last time, he opened his eyes to see her. Some dear friends came by and had a private moment with Gene.

Tim Flynn, Gene's friend and successor at KPMG, came to say good-bye.

———◦———

In the afternoon, Gene said to me, "Most people do not have the right mind or body to be able to die consciously."

As always, I was deeply interested in what he was trying to communicate. Finally I was able to understand that to him, mind meant mental discipline and body meant soul.

I asked Gene if he was prepared to leave me.

"I think so," he replied. I told him not to hang on and assured him I would be all right. He had entered into the final stage of his transition. He was ready to go.

———◦———

Less than three hours later, at 8:01 in the evening of Saturday, September 10, my husband died. He threw another pulmonary embolism, which the doctors said is one of the best ways to go, under the circumstances. Essentially, the embolism cuts off the oxygen supply to the brain—the mind just shuts down, then the body does. It is considered one of the quickest and least traumatic ways to leave. At the moment of death, Gene was surrounded by four women, each of whom had had medical training: Gene's sister Rose, my sister Darlene (who'd been an ICU nurse for 20 years), the night-duty nurse, and me. It was good not only for Gene to have had that, but that we women had each other.

———◦———

As prepared as we all were for the passing, the moment was still tense. I'd never witnessed someone die this way— of a pulmonary embolism—and my only concern was that Gene not feel the fear that accompanies asphyxiation. Rose knew all about it, so she could talk me through the stages. She was comforted by the peace of the passing: the numerous deaths she had witnessed in hospitals had almost all been traumatic.

Now that Gene's journey was over, I was somewhat relieved. I felt numb the rest of the evening. Rose, Darlene, and I waited for Gene to be taken away. Afterward, we sat in the kitchen and drank one of Gene's favorite bottles of wine and talked about what we had all experienced.

The next morning, I felt sublime joy and tranquility. The pain of loss would set in later. This was a time of celebration. Gene had left in peace. I looked out at the river and saw the sunlight glittering on the water.

It was a perfect moment.

———◦———

The funeral was beautiful, everything Gene had wanted. Several hundred people attended—family, friends, colleagues, admirers. Gene had touched many people in his brief life. My sister Darlene and I had taken great care in planning the service. The harpist and flutist played sublime music, particularly "Dance of the Blessed Spirits." The three eulogies were moving and unique: Each speaker—Tim

Flynn, Stan O'Neal, and Gene's brother William—spoke about different qualities of Gene. Stan recalled how Gene had written him a letter requesting that he give one of the eulogies; since Stan didn't receive the letter until after Gene was gone, "even if I wanted to protest," said Stan, "I couldn't." Those in the church laughed, a welcome release. The wake afterward was overflowing and had a joyous, celebratory feeling—exactly what Gene had hoped for.

————

During the last days of his life, Gene worked hard at dying. When he was awake, he focused on what he was doing. Gene had always worked hard at everything, but it was during these last 72 to 96 hours or so that I gained a new level of respect for his fortitude. I imagined it was as if he was in labor for three or four days—an exhausting experience for everyone around, but almost unfathomably taxing for the person doing it, focused on that one thing.

I also couldn't help but compare it to how hard it is to stay focused on hitting a golf ball. The very best shots are hit when you visually focus on one little spot on the ball. You do not let your eyes move. You do not let your focus move. You do not think, "I'm going to hit it straight" or "I'm not going to slice." You must get to a point where you just swing and hit it. It's very hard to concentrate that hard for five seconds. Try doing it for three or four days on end.

————

There are things that could have been done differently, of course, as there always are. While we embarked on radiation hoping to shrink the tumors and thus reduce some of the symptoms, I wondered afterwards if sticking with the process for the entire six weeks had been the right decision. The whole left side of Gene's brain was being irradiated, meaning that everything controlled by that hemisphere (the right side of the body) was affected by the treatment. Was the steep decline in Gene's condition hastened by such extensive treatment? Could we have achieved a better balance between containing his symptoms, on one hand, and preserving his functioning, on the other? I don't know. There are trade-offs with everything.

Then again, the radiation experience turned out to be a great gift. After trudging every day for six weeks to the clinic, where he saw and met so many cancer patients less fortunate than he—those who were poorer, or lacking the personal support he had, or were too timid to say something when a machine broke or they were being ignored, or too confused and scared about their inability to help plot a future for their family that might not include them— Gene set up a charitable giving fund, the Eugene O'Kelly Cancer Survivors' Fund, to provide financial help for people in need of cancer care.

Although there were perhaps misjudgments, too, in some aspects of the unwindings, the overall pursuit of unwinding was important and right. The nature of the unwindings changed as Gene (or anyone) got closer to the center of the circle; while "perfect" exchanges can happen for many in the outer rings, for those closest to you, there is no single gesture that really allows you to say good-bye to each other. This is analogous to what was happening with Gene (or might happen with almost any individual): There are important layers of personality on the outside, but at the center is the soul, a far more rich and complex essence. The letting go of attachments differs as you close in on the center of the circle because your relation to those individuals is intricately woven into the center of your being. These relationships can only be "unwound" successfully when both people can let go. It is difficult and painful. It was my deep love of Gene that enabled me to encourage him to go. Today, if he appeared before me, I would not be so strong.

As to the unwinding with Gina: Gene had worked so hard to find the perfect trip or gesture or gift for her to have the rest of her life . . . but how was that ever possible? How do you unwind a relationship with a child? Your child? Who's 14 years old? He was so goal-oriented and optimistic and such a doer, he was convinced that somewhere out there an encouragement actually existed that would do the trick. But I told him I thought it was an inherently impossible task. Gene—being Gene—kept thinking about what he needed to do or say, even though he'd done and said everything he needed to . . . had she been an adult. All the ingredients were there, from him to her. But he could never satisfy himself that he'd done it right with her because he lacked the one final ingredient he couldn't summon, no matter how hard he tried.

Time.

Some may wonder why Gene wanted to reach the highest level of consciousness possible at the time of his death. Gene believed that by achieving such a state, he would come closest to embracing his soul, the divine spirit within all of us. What better way to bridge this world and the next than to be as close to the divine as possible? He believed that if you were in touch with your divine self, then there really was no bridge to cross. This not only required practice and concentration, but necessitated his letting go of all the attachments he had developed throughout his life. It's this idea that motivated the unwindings.

By committing himself to the greatest possible consciousness at the worst, most difficult time, he also set an example for all of us who witnessed it. For our family, it reaffirmed, more intensely than ever, the power of working together toward a goal, how truly the sum can be greater than the parts. When you're living your everyday life, with no sword dangling over you, it's easy to get lost in your own orbit, as does everyone else. When you're living an extraordinary life, however, the way we all were for that incredibly long, incredibly brief season from late May through early September, you come to understand awe. You come to understand strength, commitment, love, and, most important, *life* in a way that humbles you.

It was the last thing he could do for us. In plotting out his last days the way he did, he made a dreadful experience as positive as it could be for his daughters, his wife, our family, our friends, his firm. Every calculated step was filled with truth of purpose. He made sure all our affairs were in order. From practically the moment the diagnosis was confirmed, he completely let go of work, the work he had loved at the firm he had loved—a gesture, first and last, inspired by love: It made it so much easier on the firm and its people. And when he conceived of the idea for this book, a book he hoped could explore a better way to die, then spent hours and hours writing his increasingly illegible notes on legal pads, then having the notes typed up (he could no longer do it himself), then seeking out a publisher, he knew perfectly well that his fundamental limitation—his inability to be around for the book's completion—would mean I would have to work on it, too, giving us one last project together in a lifetime of meaningful projects together—our family, our home, his career.

For Marianne, his strength at the end reaffirmed the idea that to go through life not fully awake is not to really live. By gliding along, you do the world and yourself no favors. His example showed that you can always push a little harder, be a little better. She feels it will make her a better person and parent, and she intends to stress that ideal to her children.

For Gina, no aphorisms or explanations will diminish any time soon the pain she feels, and even this book, this chronicle of her father's last and, in many ways, best (and certainly most available) couple of months, may do precious little to alleviate it. He is gone, after all. But in trying to make the best of things, trying to make something new of dying that might lead to an even better place, and the encouragement and confidence implicit in such an endeavor—that, in my opinion, is the greatest gift her dad gave her. It makes me glad to think that if her father could face life that way, his namesake can, too.

For me? Among many other things I gained from the experience—profound feelings and insights, but ones still too fresh for me to articulate here—Gene did this: While he may have left me (to use his preferred metaphor) on the golf course as we were chasing daylight, he sure teed it up for me nicely for the remainder of the round.

Gene wasn't the only one who used these trying and special months to be as clear and focused as possible. I, too, was focused on keeping him on his path, while also providing support for our daughters.

Now that he's gone and I must cope without him, I will be aided by this same trust in clarity and focus—at the end, of course, but also for each and every single day until then.

AFTERWORD

By now you have read a story that, I hope, will have the power to forever change the way you approach life and, consequently, death. It is a story that documents the partnership of me and my husband, Eugene O'Kelly. Following Gene's diagnosis, we realized that our approach had to be different from most—that getting through this would mean utilizing all the lessons and experiences we had shared together in the past. You see, Gene and I were the ultimate teammates: Our collaboration, focus, reflection, and sheer hard work over those years were as meaningful as they were satisfying. And although no one looks forward to the prospect of dying, Gene and I found a way to employ our existing skills and implement them to face our biggest challenge—the diagnosis of terminal cancer.

As I am sure you can gauge after reading this memoir, Gene was always moving at 100 miles an hour. He worked *all* the time. For the two-plus years that Gene had been CEO of KPMG, our teamwork was honed to an all-time high. It had to be because Gene bore responsibility for thousands of lives and billions of dollars he managed. Little did we know that we were primed to deal with a situation of catastrophic proportions.

As we faced Gene's diagnosis, we applied the tools we learned over past decades to make the last 100 days of his life a *personal* success. It is my hope that this book has allowed you to think about what it means to accept death and enjoy every moment you have.

People often tell me that what they admired most about Gene was his strength. What they don't always know is that Gene's strength came from a lifetime of mastering lessons in his personal and professional world. We took every experience, good or bad, as a lesson. Gene and I realized early on that the ability to see the big picture was a higher order of thinking and more important than commitment to a specific value or goal. From the well of experiences we shared over our time together, there seemed to be five prominent messages that helped prepare us for any situation. I'd like to take a moment to share these life pillars with you in the hope that they will be as helpful to you as they were for Gene and me.

The first lesson is to *face reality*

When Gene was younger, he had an insatiable need for control. He needed to feel that he had authority over particular situations so he could execute them as successfully as possible. This is a common characteristic among CEOs and probably why Gene was an outstanding leader. However, when Gene found about his cancer, it was a major turning point in his life (for the obvious reasons) but also because there was nothing he could do to rid his body of the disease. He could fight for lofty radical treatments, keep himself in a state of denial, or just face reality. Facing reality is living precisely in this moment, right now, with as much awareness as we are capable of. And it means distinguishing between what we can exert influence over and what we can't. Gene knew that he could not let his emotions or his will get in the way of accepting what was fact. When we came home from the doctor's office the day of his diagnosis, we immediately began planning for the final phase of his life.

The second lesson is to *simplify*

Simplifying means that it's necessary to discriminate among short-, medium- and long-term goals and to let go of what no longer serves us. It is simplifying that helps us take a step back from the minute details and focus on the big picture. Our culture is innovative and fast-paced and often involves multitasking. As a result we have become addicted to better and more—which usually means more complex. For example, at the end Gene looked around and noticed that many of his friends seemed to be pursuing "more" without asking themselves, "What is enough?" This question haunted him. Is an expensive car or a private jet really what you want when your personal life is a train wreck? The key here is figuring out your highest priorities first and working to attain them.

The third lesson is to *live in the moment*

After receiving his diagnosis, Gene discovered an important reason to be in the moment. With only months to live and every last moment precious, Gene discovered that time slowed down. By enjoying each moment for exactly what it was, Gene gained a new respect for, well, everything. I think the idea of living in the moment is also why Gene changed his "king of virtues" from commitment to consciousness. When we take an active interest in focusing on the present, it centers us. When we are able to take thorough stock of the present—being as precise and attentive as possible—we have more information, and more reality-based information, to think with, and this is a highly prized commodity.

The fourth lesson is *recognizing perfection*

Gene spent a lifetime thinking critically—evaluating outcome probabilities instead of outcome possibilities. Then
he learned the joy of recognizing what can be perfect in
a moment. When he woke up, he was excited and could-
n't wait to see what the day would hold. Within hours of
receiving Gene's diagnosis, I decided that I did not want
to look back with regret after Gene was gone. I didn't
want to think I had wasted any of the 100 days we had
left. We decided then and there to focus on creating
meaningful moments—perfect moments—that we could
share with the important people in Gene's life. These
perfect moments included letters, phone calls, walks in
the park, fabulous meals, and even intimate conversations
from a hospital bed. What we created was a bank account
of perfect moments for ourselves and for others. It still is
ironic to me how perfection can be found in imperfection. By that, I mean that a perfect moment doesn't have
to be a pristine event on the water or in a fancy restaurant; it can be as simple as a shared glance or just taking a
step back to laugh at yourself.

The fifth lesson is *achieving balance*

Most people have decades to prepare for the inevitable.
I knew Gene was faced with a 100-day deadline. How

many of us are faced with 100-day deadlines and get it right?

With this in mind, within hours of his diagnosis I told Gene that he had better start preparing for his death. I had been through this before, and I knew what he would be facing. I knew that his ability to stay centered would be absolutely crucial. We began experimenting with ways to facilitate his being able to be intensely focused from a balanced perspective. We did a little experimenting and found that the garden at the Cloisters (a medieval museum in Manhattan) was the perfect place for Gene; the sound of the water was exactly what he needed. The result was that every major idea of how Gene was going to spend the last 100 days of his life came out of our sessions at the Cloisters. And we didn't spend an inordinate amount of time to achieve this, perhaps two hours a week at most.

An important point to this story is that dedicating time to achieving balance was a dynamic and collaborative activity. Our time at the Cloisters, though, was the natural extension of what we had always done throughout our marriage: seek balance, collaborate, reflect, and plan. Sometimes we did it over a bottle of wine, sometimes on a chairlift, sometimes at St. James Church, and, ultimately, at the Cloisters. We talked about our goals and gave each other progress reports. It was an integral part of our life that set the framework for how we handled any sort of obstacle in our lives.

The combined impact of these lessons is enormously powerful. When we face reality, simplify, stay in the moment, recognize perfection, and achieve balance, we improve our chances of creating a life we enjoy living right now:

❖ When facing reality, we want to see the big picture.

❖ To simplify, it's important to consider all aspects of our experience.

❖ The experience of being in the moment centers us, and being centered puts us in the moment.

❖ Recognizing perfection requires us to notice where we are at any given moment. If we are in the center, also look to the periphery. Likewise, if we are on the periphery, recognize where the other rings are and where the center is.

❖ Achieving balance is the ability to be centered wherever we are. Ideally, we want to increase the size of the center so that it encompasses as many rings as possible.

Gene and I knew from 30 years of teamwork that successful people have to be very efficient and make decisions wisely, learning from every experience. Although Gene had to leave his position as CEO for KPMG, he took on a much more challenging, yet rewarding position—becoming the CEO of his death. Although that may sound morbid, it is actually a very empowering thing. By using the skills and tools we had acquired through our lives together, we learned how to adapt in the face of adversity. You could say that we were putting our knowledge to the ultimate test—and we passed.

Chasing Daylight
by Eugene O'Kelly

———◦——◦———

A READER'S GUIDE

———◦——◦———

Chasing Daylight
QUESTIONS FOR
DISCUSSION

1. In section 1, "A Gift," O'Kelly mentions that prior
   to his diagnosis, his thoughts before going to bed
   every night centered around things that were to
   happen months later; O'Kelly went on to say that
   his role as CEO for a major corporation afforded
   him the ability to take heed of the "big picture."
   In your own opinion, what other skills in O'Kelly's
   professional life prepared him for his ultimate
   lesson in dying?

2. In the opening pages of *Chasing Daylight*, O'Kelly
   confesses that he sacrificed inordinate amounts of
   time with his family to build a better future in the

long run. O'Kelly says that this turns out to be one of his biggest laments, but believed he was doing what was best for his family. This is a common thread in American thinking. Have we, as a society, become so career-driven that we have lost sight of our ability to balance a successful professional life with our personal lives? What is the best way to achieve this balance?

3. In keeping with this theme, Gene says (Section 4, "The Best Death Possible") that one solution is to expend less *time* and exert more *energy*. However, on page 78, he also mentions that this can become a problem because corporate America measures commitment by how many hours one outputs. Discuss your position on this. Do you agree or disagree with Gene? Is simply exerting more energy enough? What is the solution for those who are operating at peak performance but struggle to achieve success in their personal lives?

4. O'Kelly states that neither he nor Corinne ever ran from his diagnosis. It was something they saw as inevitable, and so they approached the situation knowing what the end result would be. O'Kelly said it is for this reason that he did not pursue any sort of radical treatment: "Some friends and

colleagues seemed almost offended by my attitude and chosen course, as if I has laid bare the fact that miracles, or their possibility, were ultimately worth rejecting." Gene made the decision to accept death. Some would argue that this meant that he accepted defeat, while others say he looked at the situation realistically, saw that there was no hope for a cure, and decided to spend his remaining time in peace, rather than trying radical treatments. Do you agree with Gene's decision? What would you do in this situation?

5. As a culture, do we take enough time to consider our own death? In Gene's own words, "I came to wonder, almost marvel, over this question: If how we die is one of the most important decisions we can make, then why do most people abrogate this responsibility?" Is this something that is a problem in other cultures as well? How do we start the process of changing how we look at death?

6. Throughout the book, Gene discusses the importance of living in the present. However, for most of us, our lives have continuously been built on planning for the future. Obviously to some degree, we must plan for the future, but what are some suggestions for how to enjoy the moment?

7. "Before my illness, I had considered *commitment* king among virtues. After I was diagnosed, I came to consider consciousness king among virtues." What is your own king among virtues?

8. In section 5, "The Good Good-Bye," O'Kelly shows us a diagram of how he set out to say his good-byes. His method was to create a six-tier circle, with the innermost circle consisting of wife, followed by children, immediate family, lifetime friends, close business associates, and people met through shared experiences. Gene's plan was to start at the outside of the circle and work his way to the center. He felt that the most impactful relationships should be saved until the end. Some suggest that Gene should have reversed this order because there was no telling how soon his time would be up. Which method would you use and why?

9. Gene says that he tried to make the process of saying his good-byes (*unwindings*, as he called them) as special as possible. "They couldn't merely be the last in a series of encounters. There had to be something about each that made it stand out, that compensated for the sad premise that lay just beneath the surface. I would make sure that the

setting for our last encounter together was full of pleasure and pleasures." Gene and Corinne called these Perfect Moments and describe the importance of creating these moments. What would be your own Perfect Moment? Is it something that is engineered, or is it spontaneous? Describe.

10. As a follow-up to question 8, Gene mentioned that once he had his unwindings with each person, we would tell each: "I'd like this to be it. I set this up specifically so we could unwind. And we made a perfect moment out of this. Let's take that and go forward. Let's not schedule another one. Trying to improve on a perfect moment never works." Considering the degree of finality that Gene wanted after his unwindings, do you think his response was a bit abrupt, or was it better to close the relationship on a positive note?

11. Gene said that the one thing that always put him at ease was the water, not because he grew up as a swimmer or had any particular affinity to it, but because being near it put him at ease. "Looking at it and listening to it helped to quiet my mind, which aided my imagination of the present moment—or, more accurately my quieter mind

could move my thoughts to the next state,
whatever that was . . . because water, in its fluidity
and frictionlessness, seemed by *nature* transitional."
Is there a particular object or element that puts
you at ease the way water did for Gene?
Describe.

12. At the completion of reading Gene's story, did
    your outlook on death change? If so, in what
    way? If not, what is the biggest take-away you
    received from reading *Chasing Daylight*?

A CONVERSATION WITH CORINNE O'KELLY

———◦◉◦———

What was Gene like? What kind of man was he?

To me, the man the world knew was just the tip of the iceberg. Gene was not pretentious, had a great sense of humor, was a man's man, and in business was highly ethical. Besides all these, and other well-documented characteristics, Gene was deeply intuitive (he learned to make this a conscious trait as he matured) and deeply spiritual as well. His spiritual side was shared primarily with me.

In the book, Gene was so calm and courageous in the face of a devastating diagnosis. Was there ever a moment when he was angry or afraid of what was happening to him?

Gene exhibited the normal range of emotions, but he did not give in to them, meaning that he put a check on them if they were negative, such as with anger as he saw anger as a waste of his precious time. Fear was the only emotion that I saw Gene truly struggle with.

Two examples illustrating how Gene dealt with his emotions are (1) when we first received his diagnosis, and (2) how he dealt with the probable length of time left to him. Within two hours of receiving the news, we realized we did not want to waste any of the time we had remaining. From that moment on, Gene was able to effectively modulate his emotions. (He was far better at it than I.) Fear was the only emotion that I could see Gene struggle with. Gene was not afraid of dying, but he was afraid he would go before he could complete everything he wanted to. As time progressed, at times Gene would unrealistically lengthen the amount of time left to him.

Gene was extremely systematic in how he chose to say good-bye to his friends, beginning with the most casual acquaintances first and then moving in to more and more intimate relationships. Was it difficult for him to do this?

Gene demonstrated a remarkable ability to let go of his attachments, his colleagues, friends, and work (I assume we are not referring to inner-circle relationships.) In fact, when he made the decision to pass on the chairmanship,

I asked him if that by some miracle he got better, whether or not he would want to continue working. His response, "I am done with that; I would never go back to working like that again."

Gene writes a great deal in the book about living in the moment, in the present. He also describes how difficult that was for him. Did it change him significantly in your eyes as he began to change the way he looked at everything?

First I must say that there was constancy to who and what Gene and I were to each other; however, this was one of the areas where there was definitely a role reversal in our relationship. Having raised two daughters consecutively, I had spent more time living in the present—an inherent aspect of childhood psychology.

When Gene became ill, not only did I want to maximize our moments together, but I needed to begin to shift into the double role I am now fulfilling as well as manage his medical care—as Gene let go of his responsibilities, I began to take on more. This dynamic made it very difficult for me to live in the moment. Giving Gene the freedom to live in the moment was one of the last gifts I could give him.

You wrote in the epilogue that there was intense love in the burden of sharing this experience. Can you tell us more about that?

My end goal was that I wanted Gene to have a conscious, loving, and peaceful death. In order to accomplish this, it was necessary for him to let go of his attachments and become as centered as possible. This was a personal journey, and thus he could only do it in his own way. At times it was maddening for me, especially when I was stretched beyond capacity as well as when I saw clearly that he had less time than he thought. The whole experience, however, was grounded in our love and respect for each other. A heightened awareness of our deep spiritual bond sustained both of us throughout the experience.

While Gene successfully unwound his life, you wrote that saying good-bye to you and the children could never be completely done. Did Gene feel that way also?

Gene was looking for a way to have a sense of completion in his relationships; he wanted to feel like he had done everything he could in each circumstance so that he could leave peacefully. Those left behind are faced with something more complex. Gene felt he reached a level of mutual completion with his older daughter, Marianne. The book was the ultimate gesture that Gene had in mind for his younger daughter, Gina, though he knew it would take years before she had come to terms with losing her father.

Gene was greatly upset that his health began failing and he could not take his daughter Gina on a trip to Prague. Why was this particular gesture so important to him?

Gene attempted to communicate his love and caring to certain individuals with specific gestures. For Gina he felt he owed her an adventure. He thought if he could take her to Prague and live until Christmas, she would be better prepared to lose him.

Do you ever get closure after losing someone like Gene? Or do you just learn to go on?

What Gene and I shared and what we both became as a result of knowing each other is far greater than the loss of him. This is my closure and a source of strength.

What do you hope readers will take away from Chasing Daylight?

At the very least, this book will hopefully open more fully the dialogue on a relatively taboo subject in our culture—the process of dying. If people have an idea of what they will ultimately face, they can better structure their lives today to, dare I say, position themselves to face this transition. At the very most, this book illustrates that a peaceful, and, yes, beautiful death is possible.